T0326984

GREAT

DISCOVER THE GREAT PLAINS

Series Editor: Richard Edwards, Center for Great Plains Studies

KENNETH F. DEWEY

PLAINS

Weather

UNIVERSITY OF NEBRASKA PRESS   *Lincoln*

A Project of the Center for Great Plains Studies, University of Nebraska

Library of Congress Cataloging-
in-Publication Data
Names: Dewey, Kenneth F. (Kenneth Frederic),
1947– author. | University of Nebraska–
Lincoln. Center for Great Plains Studies.
Title: Great Plains weather / Kenneth F. Dewey.
Description: Lincoln: University of Nebraska
Press, [2019] | Series: Discover the Great Plains
| "A Project of the Center for Great Plains
Studies, University of Nebraska." | Includes
bibliographical references and index.
Identifiers: LCCN 2018052332
ISBN 9781496215499 (pbk.: alk. paper)
ISBN 9781496216335 (epub)
ISBN 9781496216342 (mobi)
ISBN 9781496216359 (pdf)
Subjects: LCSH: Storms—Great
Plains. | Meteorology—Great Plains.
| Great Plains—Climate.
Classification: LCC QC857.U6 D49 2019 |
DDC 551.550978—dc23 LC record available
at https://lccn.loc.gov/2018052332

Set in Garamond Premier by E. Cuddy.

CONTENTS

ILLUSTRATIONS

My Road to the Great Plains

From my earliest memories of growing up in Evergreen Park, Illinois, a suburb that bordered the southwestern edge of Chicago, I have always been fascinated by the variety of extreme and severe weather.

My earliest memories include the many times that I would get out of bed in the middle of the night to watch lightning in the distance as storms approached the Chicago area. I remember several times as a child playing outside during the day on summer vacation but having to come inside the house as thunderstorms moved over my neighborhood. I was convinced that the rain would come down more intensely immediately after hearing thunder in my neighborhood. No one in my family knew if this was true and my teachers looked at me strangely when I asked them about this observation. It wasn't until later, when I was in graduate school, that I read in the scientific literature that there was a connection between lightning and increased rainfall that supported this observation. I remember saying out loud, "I knew that was true."

On Sunday afternoon, March 5, 1961, I stood at the front door of my house, mesmerized by a sky that was churning with a continuous roar of thunder as lightning sprayed down throughout my neighborhood. I got more and more excited, yelling at the top of my lungs, "Whoa!" with each flash of lightning

1. An early photo with my parents in front of my house in Evergreen Park, Illinois, I was only five years old at the time, but already interested in weather. Courtesy of the author.

and almost instantaneous crash of thunder. My parents had family over for a visit and my outbursts were clearly disturbing their conversations. Finally, Mom ordered me to take my noisy enthusiasm upstairs to my bedroom. I didn't mind her directive since this would actually give me a better view of the storm! My bedroom had a view to the west and southwest and there were no trees to block my view of the sky. An appendage hanging down from the thunderstorm was rotating and moving toward my house. Not sensing any danger, I stood there fascinated by this storm that began to produce a swirling mass of clouds. A small rotating funnel cloud dropped out of the thunderstorm moving directly toward my house. This funnel passed directly over my neighborhood and, unknown to me at the time, lowered to the ground as a tornado, out of my view, several blocks east of my home. It was my first encounter with a tornado-producing storm, and it would not be my last.

The next afternoon when my father arrived home from work, he had two newspapers in his hands; looking at me very sternly he said, "Young man, we are going for a ride." He, of course, was familiar with my youthful enthusiasm and my obsession with storms. As we got into the car, he handed the two newspapers over to me, one with a huge headline, "Storm Rips City! 50 Hurt," and the second newspaper folded to page 34, which featured storm-damage photos. He smiled at me and said, "I think you will want to see this."

Many years later, on March 3, 2015, the *Chicago Tribune* newspaper, in their Ask Tom a Weather Question feature, had meteorologist Tom Skilling respond to a reader's enquiry about the March 5, 1961, tornado. Skilling noted that "this F−2 tornado killed one, injured 115, damaged or destroyed about 3,000 homes and caused total damages of about $7 million. Several injuries occurred when a café near Eighty-Seventh and Loomis was unroofed, trapping a group of diners. A man thrown against a building by the storm was the lone fatality."

We drove from Ninety-Third Street, where we lived, to Ninety-First Street and then headed east several more blocks. Suddenly, there it was in front of me. Almost all of the homes where I lived were narrow two-story brick structures and the businesses that lined the main streets were also mostly brick and would be considered substantial structures. We had suddenly come into an area where these seemingly well-built homes and businesses had been ripped apart, with bricks and roofs littering the yards and streets. Instead of being frightened by the destruction that I saw as he drove me around the neighborhood, I became even more driven to understand what would cause the weather to, as I told my dad, on that day "throw such a tantrum." I began to collect storm and extreme weather news reports from the local newspapers, starting with this event, and I put them into my weather scrapbooks.

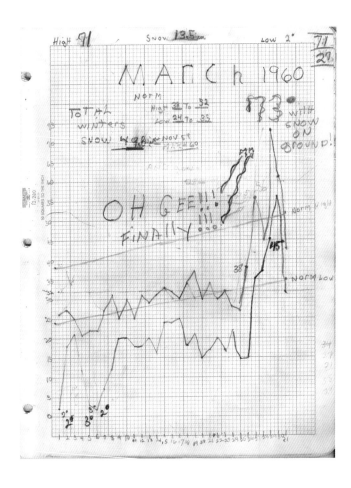

2. March 1960 graph of high and low temperatures in Chicago. My enthusiasm about weather extremes is obvious with my notation of "OH GEE, Finally!!!" put on the graph pointing at the 73° and noting that it was that warm with snow still on the ground. Photo by the author.

I never expected to see these old scrapbooks again, but when I was clearing out my mother's estate several years ago, I found that she had kept a box of keepsakes about my life including my birth certificate, school grades and awards, and my weather scrapbooks. In addition to the newspaper clippings, my weather scrapbooks contained monthly graphs where I had entered the daily highs and lows and noted any extreme weather events that had taken place during the month.

It should be noted that most boys my age were collecting baseball cards, but not me. I was collecting weather data! Little did I know at the time that I was clearly destined to have a career in climatology. Here I am five decades later and I am still producing these identical graphical products, but computers now help make the end products look much more professional. And instead of going into my weather scrapbooks, these graphs are at a University of Nebraska–Lincoln website for the public and the media to see.

I began to watch the weather reports on T V with the same dedication with which many people watch their favorite sports team. When we were on family vacations in distant locations in the U.S., I became intrigued with the regional climate differences. The most memorable trips were those taken in winter by car as I watched the dreary, cold, snow-covered landscape of my home in Chicago gradually change to a green landscape with springlike temperatures as we reached the southern states. I still, to this very day, enjoy my road trips from the center of the cold, snow-covered Nebraska landscape to the southern states during the winter. Each January my professional organization, the American Meteorological Society, has its annual meeting in various locations across the southern United States (for example, Atlanta, Georgia; New Orleans, Louisiana; Dallas, Texas; Austin, Texas; San Antonio, Texas; Phoenix, Arizona; Long Beach, California; and San Diego, California). While most of my colleagues choose to take a plane to get to these meetings, I have always enjoyed going by car and experiencing the change in climate and weather along the way.

On January 4, 2018, I headed south by car from Lincoln, Nebraska, to my annual professional meeting being held in Austin, Texas. I always look forward to my transecting of the plains, especially going south in the winter. As was usual for this time of year, and for this type of trip, we had winter parkas, hats and gloves, spring coats, and a summer wardrobe in our suitcases. It was only 5° as I pulled out of my driveway. (Note that all temperatures in this book are given in degrees Fahrenheit.) The rural landscape of southeast Nebraska was covered in snow from a recent snowfall. As we neared the Kansas-Nebraska border and the southern limit of the snow cover, the landscape took on a surreal appearance.

During the night a gentle southerly breeze with relatively mild temperatures would reach the snow cover and rapidly cool to its condensation temperature, with frost building up on all of the trees. As the air continued northward the moisture was no longer condensing out, so there was only a narrow five-mile-wide band of this frost-covered landscape.

Continuing south into Kansas, the on-board car thermometer continued to inch upward into the 20s, 30s, and then 40s. When we entered Oklahoma we began to notice green in the fields as the winter wheat sat ready to begin its springtime growth. Stopping in Blackwell, Oklahoma, to fuel up the car, I sat in the car for thirty minutes taking a break from the drive. I came to the conclusion that the Great Plains truly has two types of residents, the "northerners" and the "southerners."

The outdoor temperature was 49° but it was sunny with only a gentle wind. There were cars with license plates from Minnesota, Iowa, South Dakota, and Nebraska, with adults and children in these cars tossing their winter coats, hats, and gloves

3. January 4, 2018, Along Nebraska Highway 4, near Daykin, Nebraska, and just east of Highway 81 and Bruning, Nebraska. Photo by the author.

into the backs of their cars as they got out and headed into the nearby quick-stop store. However, there were also several cars with Texas, Arizona, and Mississippi license plates that arrived at my location, and those adults and children got out of their cars pulling their stocking caps down further, rushing into the building to get out of the "cold." One of the Texas drivers fueling his car was shivering and bouncing back and forth from one leg to the other to try to keep warm. The northerners clearly found that 49° was a pleasant and welcome change from the extreme cold to the north, yet the southerners found this temperature to be bitter cold.

This was just a small sample, and perhaps an unfounded generalization, but I chose to stop "collecting data" and continued south to Austin. By the time I reached our destination in south-central Texas, it felt like spring, with temperatures in the 60s, and a few days later it felt like early summer with temperatures approaching 80°. The return trip ten days later brought me from summer and spring weather back into the frozen North, which I wholeheartedly embraced.

Friday afternoon, April 21, 1967, is a day that I will never forget and, looking back, it ultimately influenced my decision to pursue a career on the Great Plains.

The Chicago area had its worst tornado outbreak in history on this day. Ten tornadoes slammed into northeastern Illinois, three of these tornadoes were especially violent. These ten tornadoes resulted in fifty-eight fatalities, more than one hundred injuries, and nearly half a billion dollars in damage. I was a student at Elmhurst College (located fifteen miles straight west of downtown Chicago) and majoring in geography with the goal of becoming an urban planner. As I stepped outside following my 3:30 class on April 21, 1967, I immediately felt anxious as the afternoon sky became turbulent; and it felt in so many ways like it did when I had seen my first tornado in Chicago six years earlier. I can still recall the feeling of dread as I stood outside in what felt like a sauna, and I could hear an almost continuous roar of thunder in the distance off to the south of campus. Some large raindrops (which were, as I learned later in my career, typical of melted hailstones) began to fall as the spring storm approached the college campus. The busy sidewalks on the campus quickly became deserted as students fled to their dorms or the nearby student union. I remember being the last person seeking cover, and as I entered the student union turned to two of my friends, who were watching the storm from the safety of the building, and I commented several times, "Something isn't right, that's not your ordinary thunderstorm off to our south." The storm moved east and didn't hit the campus, but as I ate dinner with a group of my friends, it was impossible to shake off that anxious feeling, even though the storm had by now moved well out of the area.

We were having an open house that evening on campus for the new science center, which housed several academic programs including the geography department. One of my physical geography professors had built a weather instrument shelter in front of the new building and I had volunteered to do the daily collection of data from that location for him. I took this responsibility very seriously and really enjoyed not only helping collect the data but producing graphs and examining the data as the data archive grew over time. I had invited my parents to come to the open house and I was looking forward to introducing them to my professors and showing them how I was helping to collect weather and climate data for the campus science center.

The open house began, but I sat on the steps out front waiting and waiting for my parents. Finally my impatience vanished as I saw them entering the nearby parking lot. But my joy quickly turned into concern as I perceived that something was terribly wrong. They looked upset and motioned for me to come over to the car. My mom was staring ahead and barely speaking, but my dad quickly related why they were upset and what they had seen while trying to come up for the open house on campus.

My dad said that as they had left their home and tried to drive through the suburb of Oak Lawn, Illinois, they found traffic was at a standstill. He related that as they looked into the distance, they saw many flashing red lights from emergency vehicles. They were diverted south away from the area and finally got onto the Tri-State Toll Road so that they could head twenty miles north to Elmhurst College. Not knowing why access to Oak Lawn, Illinois, was cut off, they had turned on the car radio and learned that about an hour earlier a tornado had moved through Oak Lawn with massive destruction. As they drove into the parking lot near the college science center, a reporter on the radio station stated that there had been mass casualties from the tornado with the worst destruction centered on the corner of Ninety-Fifth Street and Southwest Highway. This location was less than one block from my grandmother's house. Hearing this radio report was very upsetting to them, and being very worried, they said that they were immediately turning around and heading back to see if my grandmother was safe.

I did not have contact with them again until the next morning, Saturday, April 22, 1967, when they contacted me by phone at the dorm. They let me know that my grandmother was safe, her house was damaged, and that they had taken her to a relative's house after reaching her home. They knew they didn't need to ask me if I was interested and instead informed me that they were leaving to bring me down to see the tornado-damaged neighborhood of my grandmother.

During the twenty-five-minute drive to the tornado-damaged area they related in detail their experience of returning to the tornado disaster area the previous evening. When they arrived at the perimeter of the closed-off area they found that the local National Guard unit had been deployed to secure the damaged area and to keep the curious public from entering. My parents told them that my grandmother was elderly and lived alone and that they wanted to get into her neighborhood to see if she was safe. One of the guardsmen agreed to escort them into the neighborhood. My parents said it looked like a war zone. Debris was scattered everywhere, it was totally dark, and active rescues were going on trying to get people who were trapped out of crushed cars, as well as searching for victims in the nearby destroyed businesses and homes.

They had no landmarks left to know where they were relative to my grandmother's house until they reached the Sherwood Forest Restaurant, a short walking distance from my grandmother's house.

We later learned that among the Oak Lawn tornado victims, eighteen were killed in this one-square-block area of

4. Rescue workers dig through the debris of the Sherwood Forest Restaurant a few hundred yards from my grandmother's home in Oak Lawn, Illinois. Photo courtesy of NOAA/NWSCRH.

Ninety-Fifth Street and Southwest Highway, including three at the Fairway Super Mart, one at the Sherwood Forest Restaurant, three at Shoot's Lynwood Tavern, two at the Suburban Bus terminal garage, and nine in cars waiting at a red light at Ninety-Fifth Street. As they turned back toward the location of my grandmother's house, they were able to find the house but debris kept them from directly getting into the structure. My dad related that with my mom softly crying, the guardsman carried her over the debris to reach the front door of the house. They pulled debris to the side at the door and entered the first floor of the house. Much of the top floor had been destroyed and was now open to the sky.

They told me that they feared my grandmother had been killed, and they heard no sounds other than from the rescue workers in the neighborhood. My mother, convinced that my grandmother had been killed, was quite inconsolable. My dad went back out to the front door of the house and decided to at least call out her name, thinking that she might have gone to a neighbor's house or was actually outside trying to walk away from the damaged area. When he yelled, "Cora, can you hear me?" several times, a very calm but annoyed-sounding voice came back to him from under the nearby dining-room table, just inside the front door, saying, "What do you want?" A rescue worker and my dad removed debris from the top of the table and from around the table and there she was, curled up in a ball under the table with only a few scratches. She had no idea how long she had been under there and kept repeating that just before the power went out and the TV went quiet she heard them say on the TV station, "If you are in the path of the tornado get underneath something sturdy and stay there until we issue an all-clear for the area." She remained under the table waiting for the all-clear message from the TV station, not knowing that power to the house had been knocked out when the tornado tore through the neighborhood. According to my parents, she then announced that she wanted to stay in the house so that she could start cleaning up the mess. I can imagine an equally stern voice of one of the emergency management workers looking straight at her and announcing, "I don't think so, you will be coming with us." My parents realized that she was likely in shock and took her instead to a relative's house where she would be safe, warm, and have all the necessary "comforts" of an undamaged home.

As we arrived at my grandmother's neighborhood that Saturday morning, the three of us were given permission to enter the area, which was still off-limits to the curious public and only accessible by the neighborhood residents and family members who were helping with the cleanup and recovery of possessions. Before I began to help at my grandmother's house, I walked up and down her street and several surrounding streets pausing from time to time to just stare at the incredible damage. I didn't own a camera to preserve the memories, but these scenes are still vivid in my mind five decades later, returning whenever I've encountered subsequent tornado-damaged areas on the plains.

The next day, Sunday April 23, 1967, I was back on campus watching snow falling outside my dorm window. During the week leading up to the tornado outbreak, Chicago had experienced five days in a row with high temperatures in the 70s, with nearby Rockford, Illinois, reaching 80°. Now only two days after this tornado outbreak, northern Illinois was having a rare late April snowfall. A total of 3.8 inches of snow fell at Rockford, sixty miles to the northwest of Oak Lawn, and 3.2 inches of snow fell at nearby Chicago Midway Airport. This tornado event and the extreme change in weather in April 1967, from sunny and very warm to violent storms and then snowfall, was a defining moment of my life that eventually led me to a career studying the climatology of severe storms, climate extremes, storm damage, and public severe-weather preparedness education.

Anyone who knew me at the time would certainly say that I loved to talk about the weather and climate almost nonstop. Two of my closest friends at Elmhurst College, Jack and Marianne, were graduating along with me, and they were starting careers in public school teaching. One Saturday evening these two friends posed a simple question, "Why don't you get a PhD so you can be a college professor and share all of this enthusiasm with your students?" In a moment the last piece of the puzzle fell into place. Suddenly it all seemed clear, and I never looked back. After graduating with a bachelor's degree in geography from Elmhurst College, I entered graduate school. I didn't want to be a weather forecaster, but instead wanted to study the spatial variation in severe weather. This was achieved in the geography department at Northern Illinois University for my master's degree and in the geography department at the University of Toronto, in Canada, for my PhD degree.

As I neared graduation with my PhD, I applied for a job at the Atmospheric Environment Service (now called Environment Canada) office in Toronto (the equivalent of our National Weather Service in the U.S.) as well as for several academic openings across the U.S. Although I could have lived in Toronto, Los Angeles, Berkeley, Portland, Oregon, or Delaware, I was the most excited about the potential of having a teaching position at the University of Nebraska–Lincoln. I left the frozen, snow-covered landscape of Toronto and arrived for the job interview in Lincoln on February 17, 1974, where the temperature that afternoon was 62°.

When I was called a week later on February 24, 1974, and verbally offered the job, the chair of the geography department told me that it was barely above zero (only 5°) outside and that strong winds were whipping the snowfall that Lincoln had just received into blizzard conditions. I received the official job offer in the mail, signed the form, and immediately returned it to the University of Nebraska. One week later, on March 2, I received another phone call from the chair of the geography department confirming my starting date. I was to begin my career on the Great Plains at the University of Nebraska–Lincoln. As he was ready to conclude the phone call, I asked, "Out of curiosity, what is the weather like today in Lincoln?" He responded in a nonchalant manner, "Oh its 76° and it feels like summer." Realizing that in a two-week period, Lincoln had gone from sunny mid-60s to near zero and a blizzard and then back up to the mid-70s, I knew that the Great Plains was a location of fascinating weather extremes.

During the following summer of 1974, my parents gathered the family together for a large farewell party for me as I prepared to leave the Chicago suburbs and live in Nebraska. Toward the end of the evening, family members were sharing stories and wishing me well. I clearly remember every word that my Aunt Barbara said. She sighed loudly, shook her head, and, with a furrowed brow, looked at me and said, "Are you sure you want to go to Nebraska? Don't they have blizzards, tornadoes, heat waves, tornadoes, dustbowls, cold waves, AND tornadoes there?" She obviously was the most concerned about tornadoes. Undeterred, I smiled and enthusiastically replied, "Yes, that's exactly why I am going there!" And with that, I made the best choice of my life to pursue my career path. I was taking the road to Nebraska and the Great Plains, where I could spend a lifetime surrounded by weather extremes.

There is a wealth of information about the Great Plains weather and so many stories that could be told. Although it was difficult to narrow down the topics for this book, I have chosen the six topics that I thought would be the most familiar to the residents of the Great Plains and the most interesting for the readers who are not familiar with the variety of extreme weather that we experience here on the plains. There are numerous approaches to delineating the boundaries of the Great Plains. The definition used in this book is shown on a map that was acquired from the *Encyclopedia of the Great Plains* (edited by David J. Wishart) as well as Lavin, Shelley, and Archer's *Atlas of the Great Plains*.

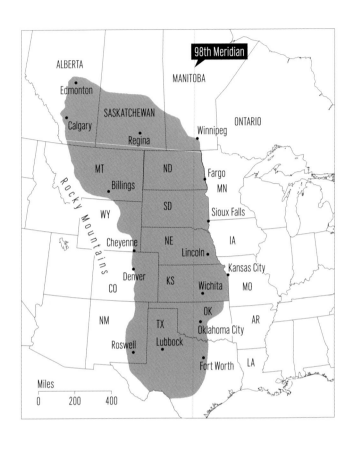

5. Map of the Great Plains redrawn by Katie Nieland from the map by Clark Archer in *Atlas of the Great Plains*.

GREAT PLAINS WEATHER

CHAPTER ONE

The Heartland of Weather and Climate Extremes

Most areas of the United States can claim that they "own" their local climate. For example, much of Colorado has a "mountain" climate, New England has a "cool maritime" climate, the Gulf region has a "warm humid tropical" climate, the Southwest has a "desert climate," and even northern Minnesota refers to their area as the "Icebox of America." I contend that the Great Plains doesn't own its own climate, but instead borrows heavily from all of the climates outside our region. When I ask residents of the Great Plains to describe their climate, I often hear such words and phrases as "extreme," "windy," "changeable," "four contrasting seasons," "unpredictable weather," "constantly changing weather," "never boring or monotonous," "intense," and so on.

I knew about the extremes in weather and climate in the Great Plains before I decided to move here from Chicago, so I was especially excited to live right in the middle of the Great Plains in Nebraska. Nebraska is located near the center of the conterminous United States and is at the crossroads of contrasting air masses that approach the state from all directions. Air masses pass over the central Great Plains but never linger for very long.

The physical geography of the Great Plains, in general, is one of a gently rolling surface without any major obstructions to block advancing air masses. There are also no large water bodies

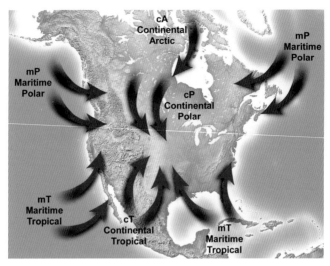

6. The five primary air mass source regions with Nebraska at the crossroads of their air mass trajectories. Map created by the author.

to modify air masses as they move across the region. No wonder, then, that the most characteristic feature of the Great Plains is the extremes in weather and very rapidly changing weather conditions. I was watching the weather forecast on a local T V channel during my first winter here in Nebraska. I recall the weathercaster saying, "It was a mild day today in Nebraska, but look at the below-zero readings this afternoon in southern Canada. Arctic cold air has begun to plunge southward across the plains and the only thing that is in its way are a few fences, and it appears they have left the gates open."

For me, that described the plains perfectly, nothing to stop extreme temperature changes from taking place and taking place quickly.

As the years rolled by, I began to say that Nebraska has a "Goldilocks principle" climate. That is, it doesn't stay hot for too long nor does it stay cold for too long and it doesn't stay

Average annual precipitation along I-80

LOCATION	INCHES
NEW YORK CITY, NY	46.23
LINCOLN, NE	28.95
SACRAMENTO, CA	18.51

Average annual days with precipitation along I-80

LOCATION	DAYS
NEW YORK CITY, NY	120
LINCOLN, NE	90
SACRAMENTO, CA	45

Average number of days with highs of 90° or more

LOCATION	DAYS
DULUTH, MN	2
FARGO, ND	13
GRAND ISLAND, NE	36
LINCOLN, NE	42
DALLAS, TX	103
AUSTIN, TX	106

Average number of days with lows of 32° or less

LOCATION	DAYS
DULUTH, MN	181
FARGO, ND	175
GRAND ISLAND, NE	146
LINCOLN, NE	143
DALLAS, TX	27
AUSTIN, TX	24

Average annual snowfall

LOCATION	INCHES
DULUTH, MN	86.1
FARGO, ND	50.1
GRAND ISLAND, NE	29
LINCOLN, NE	26.9
DALLAS, TX	1.2
AUSTIN, TX	.4

7. The Great Plains' weather sweet spot. Data source: High Plains Regional Climate Center (XMACIS archive). Created by Alexa Horn.

8. Southeast Lincoln, Nebraska, December 30, 2009, near 0° and with a deep snow cover. Photo by the author.

cloudy and rainy for too long or cloudless and too dry for too long. My perception is that anywhere on the Great Plains would be an exciting place to live due to the extremes in weather and climate that occur there; however, I think Nebraska has just the right balance in extremes and has been the perfect location for me to live, work, and play.

But looking at just the averages hides the extremes that can occur. Figures 8 and 9 illustrate the extreme contrasts that can take place on the plains. On December 30, 2009, temperatures were below zero with a deep snow cover. The same day and location, one year later, and it was warm, in the 60s, and dry.

Annual Temperature Extremes: Winter Cold, Summer Heat

The climate of the Great Plains is controlled by more than just the contrast in air masses that move across the region. The extreme climate of the plains is also the result of a physical process known as "specific heat." Specific heat plays a pivotal

9. Southeast Lincoln, Nebraska, December 30, 2010, 60° and no snow. Photo by the author.

role in the climatology of daily to annual temperatures. Dry air and dry land surfaces with a low specific heat, on average, heat and cool five times faster than relatively moist air and surfaces. Humid locations also have a much higher frequency of cloudy conditions, which means incoming solar radiation is partially blocked during the day, keeping those locations from warming very much, and at night, the clouds act as a blanket reducing night time cooling. Anyone visiting a normally humid location would observe that the air temperature does not vary much from day to night or throughout the year. The Great Plains, located far from the moderating influence of the oceans and with its typically drier and frequently cloud-free skies, experiences some of the greatest temperature contrasts observed in North America.

Bismarck, North Dakota, at latitude 46.8° north, is 3,229 miles from the North Pole and 2,981 miles from the equator. Despite being almost midway between these two extreme climatic regions, North Dakota has seen winter cold temperatures that rival polar latitudes and summer temperatures as warm as the equatorial region. The statewide record low for North Dakota is -60°, which rivals the all-time extreme low temperatures that have been observed well to the north in the Arctic. Even as far south as Texas, the record lowest temperature for the state is -23°, "Arctic" in nature and well below the record-cold temperatures that are observed at the same latitude but near either of the coasts. It is not surprising, then, that the summer heat is also intense and extreme across the Great Plains. Record heat on the Great Plains is associated with prolonged dry spells or droughts in the region.

One of the most dramatic ways of demonstrating how extreme the climate is on the Great Plains is to look at the coldest temperature ever observed within a state and compare it to the warmest temperature ever observed within that same state. Texas, for example, has seen a range of 143 degrees from its

Average High Temperatures in Winter Compared to Summer

STATE	COLDEST DAY (°F)		HOTTEST DAY (°F)		TEMP. RANGE
ND	-60	2/15/1936	121	7/6/1936	181
SD	-58	2/17/1936	120	7/5/1936, 7/15/2006	178
NE	-47	12/22/1989	118	7/24/1936	165
KS	-40	2/13/1905	121	7/24/1936	161
OK	-31	2/10/2011	120	*	151
TX	-23	2/8/1933	120	8/12/1936, 6/28/1994	143

(*) July 18 & 19, 1936; Aug 10 & 12, 1936; June 27, 1994

10. Statewide record lows and record highs in the Great Plains and the temperature range between these two extremes. Created by Alexa Horn with information from the High Plains Regional Climate Center.

coldest recorded temperature of -23° to its warmest recorded temperature of 120°. This range of temperature between the two extremes actually increases going northward in the plains. The data for North Dakota show an almost unbelievable range of 181 degrees, from their coldest ever observed temperature of -60° to its hottest ever observed temperature of 121°. The only location on Earth with greater temperature extremes is found in Siberia!

And then there is boring Key West, Florida, with a coldest recorded temperature of 41° and a hottest of 97°, with a range of only 56 degrees (encompassing 123 years of data, 1895–2017). And then there is "boring" Honolulu, Hawaii, which checks in with a coldest recorded temperature of 52° and a hottest of 95°, with a range of only 43 degrees (encompassing 128 years of data, 1890–2017).

We should be proud of ourselves on the Great Plains that it doesn't take more than one hundred years for us to see these narrow temperature ranges; we can do that all in one day.

It might be assumed that the timing of the average coldest time of the year is similar throughout the Great Plains, but that is not the case. The western edge of the Great Plains normally has its coldest temperatures in late December. As you head east in the Dakotas, Nebraska, Kansas, and Oklahoma, the coldest temperatures normally occur later, toward the end of January. The reason that this occurs is that, during the winter, the polar vortex and the core of coldest air in the Arctic begin to shift eastward as Hudson Bay freezes over, pushing the coldest temperatures further east resulting in this one-month difference in the occurrence of coldest temperatures going west to east across the Great Plains.

Average High Temperatures in Winter Compared to Summer

A characteristic feature of the temperature climatology of the Great Plains is the much larger latitudinal gradient in temperatures in winter compared to summer. For example, the average January high temperature in Fargo, North Dakota, is 17° and the average January high temperature in Brownsville, Texas, is 71°, a difference of 54 degrees. However, the average July high temperature in Fargo is 72° and Brownsville is 92°, a difference of only 20 degrees. Any road trip in winter traversing the plains from north to south requires clothing ranging from winter parkas, hats, and gloves to spring/summer shorts and T-shirts. In summer however, there isn't a need for multiple-season clothing for the same trip.

Daily Temperature Extremes: All Four Seasons in One Day

Although Mark Twain famously commented that "If you don't like the weather in New England now, just wait a few minutes," I think he really meant the Great Plains. The speed at which weather can change here on the Great Plains can take your breath away.

When I first moved to the Great Plains, I frequently heard versions of Mark Twain's comment from the residents. And recently, I have seen the following comment several times on social media as an extreme version of this concept: "Ah, the Great Plains, where you can shovel snow in the morning and go swimming in the afternoon." Part of my job is providing weather and climate updates to the public at my various climate center websites as well as on social media. I will frequently say that it looks like "roller coaster weather ahead" with lots of ups and downs in the temperature expected this week.

The temperature climatology on the plains has the largest day-to-day temperature changes occurring during the winter months when there is a large latitudinal contrast in temperatures. There are no physical barriers to deflect or slow down the cold air that has accumulated in the Canadian Arctic once it begins to move southward into the Great Plains. The winter cold fronts at the leading edge of these cold Arctic air masses can sweep down the plains from the Canadian border to Texas in less than thirty-six hours. Relatively mild air can be pushed out of the way and replaced with below-zero temperatures in the northern and central Great Plains and subfreezing temperatures in the southern Great Plains all the way to the Gulf of Mexico. It is normal to see cold fronts pass through the Great Plains, but what sets these cold fronts apart from the rest of the country is the speed at which they are moving and the temperature contrast between the area immediately ahead of the front and behind the front. Climatologists, as well as the residents of the southern plains, often refer to these strong cold winds that sweep down the Great Plains from Canada as "Northers" or "Blue Northers." The subfreezing temperatures that these Blue Northers bring to the deep south of the Great Plains would seem relatively mild to northern plains residents; however, they can cause harm to the citrus crops and cause exposed water pipes to freeze in this region.

Although there are numerous examples of these winter cold winds sweeping down the Great Plains in the climate data archives, several occurrences are historically noteworthy.

March 2–3, 1904

Imagine what it must have been like living on the high plains of western Kansas on March 2, 1904, when the temperatures plummeted from summer heat to bitter winter cold in just a few hours. There were no social media updates on the changing weather, no local TV news and weather broadcasts, no Weather Channel with twenty-four-hour continuous updates, and no radio news and weather updates. This day was unusually hot for so early in the year with brisk southerly winds pushing the temperature into the mid-80s across the high plains of western Kansas. The 86° recorded on that day in Dodge City remains the record high for that day of the year at that same location some 113 years later.

As the residents of Dodge City, Kansas, fell asleep that evening, they undoubtedly left windows propped open after a day with such warm summerlike temperatures. However, just a few hours later, they were probably jolted awake and out of bed when temperatures fell 80 degrees into the single digits, with snow blowing in through their open widows. They must have wondered how this could have happened so quickly and at first probably thought it was just a dream. I would imagine many residents wondered out loud about their sanity for choosing to live on the western high plains of Kansas. While this March 1904 cold front was very impressive, there is yet another example of an even larger drop in temperature caused by a winter cold front on the Great Plains, and I was there to experience it.

January 31–February 1, 1989

In 1989 Valentine, Nebraska, experienced an almost 100-degree temperature change across two days. January 31, 1989, was a mild winter day in Valentine, with a springlike afternoon high temperature of 70°. Then an Arctic cold front passed through Nebraska moving at over 60 mph. The temperature in Valentine crashed overnight to -15° on February 1, 1989, a fall of 85 degrees in just fifteen hours. The cold air continued to intensify, and on the second day following the cold front passage the temperature fell to -26° in Valentine. This thirty-six-hour drop in temperature was an amazing 96 degrees.

To put this into perspective, the fifteen-hour temperature change of 85 degrees in Valentine is greater than the range of all temperatures ever observed in 124 years of observations (1895–2017) in Miami, Florida. Miami's hottest recorded temperature was 100° on July 21, 1942, and their coldest recorded temperature was 27° on February 3, 1917, for an absolute temperature range of "only" 73 degrees. The people living in Valentine experienced more change in temperature in fifteen hours than an entire lifetime of multiple generations living in southern Florida.

I remember this day vividly. As I drove home from working on the UNL city campus in downtown Lincoln, it was the end of January, yet it was 70° outside. I enjoyed having the car windows open and it truly felt like it was the first day of spring. I drove past Holmes Lake Park in southeast Lincoln. I could hear the laughter of children playing on the playground equipment, I saw bicycles passing by on the trail, and people were out walking their dogs. A brisk southerly wind was creating waves on the open, that is, not ice-covered, Holmes Lake. As I arrived home, the phone was ringing, and it was a colleague of mine who was about ten miles north of me and still on campus in downtown Lincoln. He said, "Hang up the phone, go outside, and hang on."

I stepped outside onto my backyard deck and I could hear a roar in the distance. A large all-white rolling cloud that seemed to be touching the ground slammed into my neighborhood.

The wind was howling and small branches began to break off of the trees. My house began to shudder and shake. A fine mist coated everything and instantly froze as the temperature fell quickly below freezing. It started to snow so hard that it was impossible to see more than just a few feet ahead. Within fifteen minutes, the snow abruptly stopped and a bright blue sky appeared, but the temperature had already fallen into the teens on its way down to near zero later that evening. The next morning, driving to work, I drove by Holmes Lake Park that had been filled with residents enjoying the springlike weather the day before. It was empty and silent now and the lake, which had had no ice on it the day before, had flash frozen across the surface. I smiled and knew I was at home in this place with a strange extreme climate.

November 11, 1911

Many of my climatology colleagues often mention the historical extreme cold wave that swept across the plains in November 1911 and has become known as the "Great Blue Norther of November 1911." This event—similar to the March 2, 1904, cold wave—would have occurred without any advance warning. A large cold air mass parked over southern Canada broke loose and began to plunge down the Great Plains early on November 11, 1911. As usual, there was nothing to slow down or deflect this dense cold air mass as it headed south across the plains. The northern plains were already seasonally chilly so the advancing cold air mass merely reinforced the preexisting cold, and temperatures fell only 30 to 40 degrees following the passage of the cold front. As the cold air mass moved into the central plains it dislodged the late summer temperatures, which had soared into the 70s in Kansas and upper 80s in Oklahoma.

The greatest impact of this November 11–12 Blue Norther was in Oklahoma, where the temperatures plunged more than

70 degrees in just twenty-four hours. The largest temperature decrease took place in Stillwater, where the temperature fell 74 degrees from 88° to 14° with the passage of this cold front. The reason that this cold front has achieved legendary status and is often mentioned by my climatology colleagues is the fact that the cold Arctic air mass shifted well off to the east of the Great Plains and impacted more populated urban locations in the Midwest where these types of occurrences are much less frequent than on the plains.

Where Do the Greatest Cold-Front Temperature Decreases in Winter Occur on the Plains?

When examining the climate data archive for the Great Plains, it becomes obvious that the greatest twenty-four-hour temperature changes caused by cold fronts have occurred in the Nebraska-Kansas-Oklahoma area and not in the northern plains of North and South Dakota or the southern plains in Texas. One reason for this is the difficulty in getting much warming into the northern Great Plains due to a snow cover that is normally present there in winter. It is also a long distance for the warm air to travel to reach this area resulting in a highly modified (cooled) warm air mass. Any cold front moving through the northern Great Plains merely reinforces the cold air that is already in place so the temperatures don't fall as much as they do in the central Great Plains. However, by the time these cold air masses reach Texas they have greatly modified (warmed) and temperature decreases are somewhat muted there as well. Nebraska to Oklahoma is just the right region in which to experience these giant-sized temperature decreases.

The map in figure 11 provides some examples of the extreme twenty-four-hour temperature changes caused by cold fronts moving through the central Great Plains:

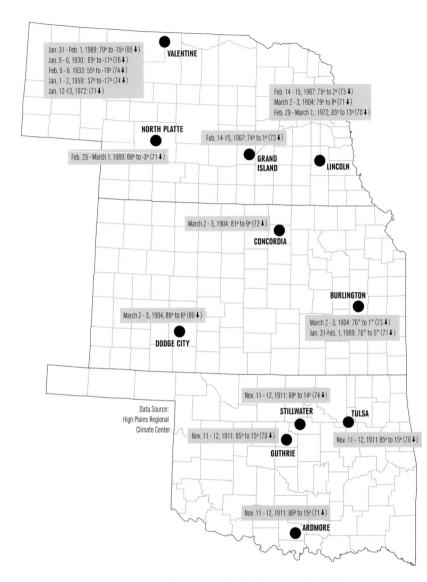

Jan. 31 - Feb. 1, 1989: 70º to -15º (85↓)
Jan. 5 - 6, 1930: 65º to -11º (76↓)
Feb. 5 - 6. 1933: 55º to -19º (74↓)
Jan. 1 - 2, 1959: 57º to -17º (74↓)
Jan. 12-13, 1972: (71↓)

VALENTINE

Feb. 14 - 15, 1967: 75º to 2º (73↓)
March 2 - 3, 1904: 79º to 8º (71↓)
Feb. 29 - March 1,: 1972, 83º to 13º (70↓)

NORTH PLATTE

Feb. 14-15, 1967: 74º to 1º (73↓)

Feb. 29 - March 1, 1989: 68º to -3º (71↓)

GRAND ISLAND

LINCOLN

March 2 - 3, 1904: 81º to 9º (72↓)

CONCORDIA

BURLINGTON

March 2 - 3, 1904, 86º to 6º (80↓)

DODGE CITY

March 2 - 3, 1904: 76° to 1° (73↓)
Jan. 31-Feb. 1, 1989: 76° to 5° (71↓)

Nov. 11 - 12, 1911: 88º to 14º (74↓)

Data Source:
High Plains Regional
Climate Center

STILLWATER

TULSA

Nov. 11 - 12, 1911: 85º to 15º (70↓)

GUTHRIE

Nov. 11 - 12, 1911 85º to 15º (70↓)

Nov. 11 - 12, 1911: 86º to 15º (71↓)

ARDMORE

11. Large temperature drops in Nebraska, Kansas, and Oklahoma. Map created by Katie Nieland with information from the High Plains Regional Climate Center.

Extreme Temperature Changes on the Plains: Setting a Record High and a Record Low on the Same Calendar Day

If these cold fronts can come through with perfect timing, it is possible that a record-high temperature can be set and then a record low temperature can be set all on the same calendar day.

Here are some examples of this strange phenomenon, from data collected from the High Plains Regional Climate Center in Lincoln, Nebraska:

Kansas City, Missouri, November 11, 1911: record high 76°, record low 11°

Oklahoma City, Oklahoma, November 11, 1911: record high 83°, record low 17°

Sioux City, Iowa, May 16, 1997: record high 91°, record low 33°

Pueblo, Colorado, July 15, 1993: record high 101°, record low 52°

The town of Alamosa, Colorado, has four days of the year that have recorded both a record high and record low on the same day. Amazingly, three of these four days occurred consecutively.

August 24, 2002: record high 85°, record low 33°

August 25, 2002: record high 87°, record low 30°

August 26, 2002: record high 88°, record low 31°

February 21, 1958: Record high 76°, record low -18°

These records remain unbroken as of the year 2017.

"Snow Eater" Winds: Extreme Temperature Changes

Some of the largest temperature changes within a twenty-four-hour period in the United States that have occurred in the high plains are not related to cold front passages, but instead have resulted from the occurrence of "Chinook" winds along the Front Range of the Rocky Mountains and the surrounding plains.

The term Chinook is claimed by popular folk etymology to mean "snow eater," but in fact the word refers to the name of the Native people in the region where the usage was first derived. Chinook winds originally meant a warming wind from the ocean coming into the interior regions of the Pacific Northwest of the United States. The Chinook people lived near the ocean and along the Columbia River. The Chinookan peoples include several groups of Indigenous people all speaking Chinookan languages. In the early nineteenth century, the Chinookan-speaking peoples resided along the lower and middle Columbia River in present-day Oregon and Washington. The Chinook tribes were those encountered by the Lewis and Clark Expedition in 1805 on the lower Columbia River.

The Chinook wind, as we use its popular definition, is a rain-shadow wind on the leeward side of a mountain. Descending air increases in pressure internally, known as the "adiabatic process," which causes air molecules to increase in their collision with each other causing a warming of the temperatures. These winds are most common during the winter months. The descending air warms at the rate of $5.5°/1,000$ feet. The descending air is a dry wind since the increasing temperatures warm the air well above the dew point or condensation temperature. Gravitational pull increases the wind speed as the air descends into the area at the bottom of the mountains. The wind speeds can reach hurricane force and the sudden warming can cause snow cover to rapidly disappear, hence the popular phrase "snow eater" winds.

The very dry air also causes a loss of snow cover due to snow directly evaporating into vapor (sublimation). It is possible to have as much as a foot of snow disappear in a day due to these Chinook winds. It is not uncommon in midwinter to sec temperatures in western Kansas and western Nebraska that are much warmer than the eastern portion of these two states as Chinook winds transition into downslope winds and push across the plains toward the Missouri River valley. And, on rare occasions, Chinook winds generated on the eastern slope of the Rocky Mountains have reached as far east as Wisconsin as they sweep across the entire Great Plains into the Midwest.

Loma, Montana, has the most extreme recorded temperature change in a twenty-four-hour period in the United States. On January 15, 1972, the temperature in the valley below the mountains had fallen to -54°. A Chinook wind kicked in and within several hours, the temperature rose to 49°, which was a 103-degree increase in temperature.

Spearfish, South Dakota, holds the world record for the fastest recorded temperature change. On January 22, 1943, at about 7:30 a.m., the temperature in Spearfish was -4°. The Chinook wind suddenly increased in velocity and, two minutes later, at 7:32 a.m., the temperature was 45°. The 49-degree temperature rise in two minutes set a world record that still holds today. By 9:00 a.m. the temperature had risen to 54°. Then, suddenly, the Chinook wind died down and the temperature tumbled back to -4°. This 58-degree drop in temperature took only twenty-seven minutes. It was reported that the sudden change in temperatures caused house windows to crack.

In early November 1993, my colleagues from across the country and I were at a meeting in Boulder, Colorado. It was colder than normal for that time of year and it snowed off and on for the first two days that we were there. During the evening of the third day, we were all in our hotel rooms in the same building. As the winds began to howl, there were repeated knocks on my hotel door and my colleagues, one by one, came in shouting "CHINOOK!" They knew that I would have the best view since I was on the top floor of the hotel and my hotel-room windows faced west into the wind and overlooked a well-lighted courtyard. A large, dense cold-air mass that had been sitting over the intermountain area of Colorado had become dislodged and was sinking out onto the plains into Boulder, with wind gusts exceeding 70 mph, and warming along the way. It wasn't long before the three-day accumulation of snowfall had disappeared in front of us. For us, watching weather and climate extremes is a form of entertainment, and best of all, it is free.

Land Hurricanes

The extreme nature of Chinooks goes beyond just the huge temperature increases to also include incredibly strong winds. Chinook winds can often be devastating with sustained winds and gusts sometimes as strong as hurricanes (over 75 mph) or even strong enough to cause damage equivalent to EF-1 (86–110 mph) and EF-2 (111–135 mph) tornadoes, uprooting trees and damaging many roofs. There are many examples of Chinooks along the Front Range of the Rocky Mountains in the data archives but one of the most extreme examples occurred on January 17, 1982, in Boulder. There were numerous reports of peak wind gusts in excess of 100 mph in the area. The Environmental Research Laboratory at the National Oceanic and Atmospheric Administration (NOAA) measured a 118-mph gust on its roof before the power failed. The National Center for Atmospheric Research (NCAR), at the highest point of Table Mesa Drive, in southwest Boulder, recorded a maximum wind gust of 137 mph just after 2:00 a.m. on the roof, six hundred feet above the city. During the second high-wind period early in the morning, NCAR recorded a 130-mph gust. In all, twenty gusts of over 120 mph were clocked at NCAR between 1:00 a.m. and 9:00 a.m. An estimated 40 percent of all buildings in Boulder received at least minor damage between the night of January 16 and the morning of January 17, 1982, and about fifty homes were damaged badly enough to be uninhabitable. In one instance, a gust completely unroofed a home, and the roof sailed over two adjacent houses before landing on a third. The winds also hit the Boulder Airport especially hard, destroying about twenty small planes. Several utility poles snapped, and thousands of electricity customers were without power. The wind also caused erosion damage to about fifty thousand acres of farmland in Boulder County.

The Strong Winds of the Great Plains

As we have seen, the extreme climate of the Great Plains can be noted in ways other than temperature and in areas of wind other than on the Front Range of the Rockies. One of the first things anyone would notice if they are visiting the plains, or if they move to the plains, is that it seems like it is a very windy location, and, in reality, it is.

When I first arrived here on the Great Plains, residents frequently commented on how windy it was throughout the year. I remember hearing someone tell me the joke that "out here on the Great Plains, it's windy even when the winds are calm." My favorite story told to me was about how "it is always so windy on the Great Plains, that one day the wind stopped and everyone fell over." Leaning into the wind is normal out here on the windswept plains.

We were in Tucson, Arizona, a few years ago in late May, staying at a resort that had a large courtyard with a morning breakfast buffet outside under the palm trees. On our sixth day of staying there, we were walking down the stairs on the way to breakfast when I said out loud to my wife, "Well here we are, another day in paradise, same weather day after day after day, same temperature, no wind, no clouds, nothing. I will be glad when we get back home." Suddenly, a man's voice behind me interrupted the morning calm saying loudly, "Us too, it just doesn't seem normal to us either, where are you from"? We stopped and, although we didn't know them, they were smiling and told us they were from western Iowa and we told

Wind Speed
m/s

>10.5
10.0
9.5
9.0
8.5
8.0
7.5
7.0
6.5
6.0
5.5
5.0
4.5
<4.0

12. The region of strongest average wind speeds encompasses primarily the Great Plains region. Redrawn at the University of Nebraska with information from the National Renewable Energy Laboratory.

them that we were from Nebraska. And guess what? We spent the next thirty minutes talking about the weather back home.

Summer Winds from Hell

Early settlers on the Great Plains used the phrase "furnace winds" or "winds from hell" to refer to the desiccating low humidity and hot summer winds that brought oppressive conditions to both humans and vegetation. Described early on as the "Great American Desert," early settlers made reference to the oppressive heat, high winds, and dry, barren plains.

A vivid account of the region survives from the 1819–20 travels of an expedition from Pittsburgh to the Rocky Mountains, recorded by James Edwin: "The wind was high, and the drifting of the sand occasioned much annoyance. The heat of the atmosphere became more intolerable, on account of the showers of burning sand driven against us."

From the same volume of Edwin's *Account of an Expedition from Pittsburgh to the Rocky Mountains*, a Signal Service observer at Leavenworth, Kansas, described the conditions on September 12, 1882: "A very hot and extremely dry wind set in from the southwest at 1pm of the 12th. At 4 pm the maximum temperature, 101°, occurred, being the highest recorded during September since the establishment of the station. The relative humidity fell to 17 percent. This hot wind continued through the remainder of the day, on the 13th and 14th. The vegetation was withered and burned up, and out-door labor was suspended."

"Furnace winds" are most frequent in the Kansas to Texas region of the Great Plains and although their frequency decreases northward from Kansas, they are still a part of the summer climate of the northern Great Plains.

It's Not Normal to Be "Normal" in the Great Plains

The question most often asked by someone moving into a new area from another distant location is "What's the weather like here?" Or "What is the normal rainfall or normal snowfall amount or normal winter or summer temperatures"? These questions imply that there must be a listing of "normal" values for the different climate elements and that these conditions could be expected to occur on a frequent basis.

Standard climate normals extend over a thirty-year period and are updated every ten years. The climate normals period referenced by this book is 1981–2010. The use of climate normals in many areas of the U.S. makes sense to get an understanding of what you might expect in weather; however, with the extremes noted earlier in this chapter, it is easy to see that it is a problem trying to define "normal" on the Great Plains.

Looking at just one calendar day—January 11—across one hundred years, from 1918 through 2017, and for Lincoln, Nebraska, not once did that location ever experience their

Observed minimum temperature

Lincoln, Neb., Jan. 11, 1918-2017

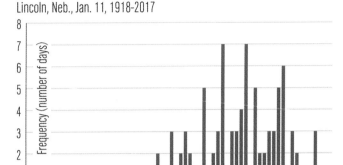

13. The "normal" January 11 low temperature in Lincoln, Nebraska, is 14°. This low temperature has never occurred during the one hundred years 1918 to 2017. Graphed with data from the High Plains Regional Climate Center.

"normal low" of 14°. And there has been a 65-degree range (from -29° to +36°) in what has been observed in low temperatures on this date over the hundred-year period. These two statistics make the concept of a "normal" low almost meaningless in Nebraska and the Great Plains.

In figure 14, with data from the High Plains Regional Climate Center, we can note that the top and bottom of each vertical blue line in the graph shows the observed highs and lows in 2016. The two curved brown lines in the middle show the normal highs and lows. The top and bottom of the red and blue lines are the record highs and lows.

There is such a huge range between the record highs and record lows on a daily basis that it is rare, not "normal," for the daily highs and daily lows to fall within the normal temperature

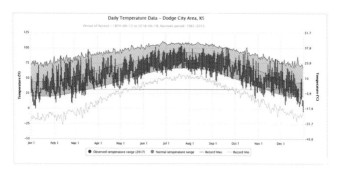

14. The observed daily high and low temperatures for Dodge City, Kansas, compared to the normal temperatures and the record highs and lows. Graphed with data from the High Plains Regional Climate Center.

range. This type of temperature distribution occurs throughout the plains, year after year.

All Four Seasons in One Month on the Plains

March is perhaps the cruelest of all months on the Great Plains, with the largest extremes in weather that are observed during the year.

March, in Nebraska, for example, has seen well-below-zero temperatures with paralyzing blizzards as well as early-summer heat with highs in the 90s. Using March 11 in Lincoln as an example, the range is 103 degrees (with a record high of 84° and a record low of -19°). It would be safe to say that during the month of March, in Nebraska, it is possible to experience all four seasons of weather. And you can easily see why telling a new resident of the central Great Plains what the "normal" March temperatures are is pointless when it can range from near 90° to well below zero.

But it's not just Nebraska. Looking at the March temperature climatology throughout the region, it is the same phenomenon from North Dakota to Texas.

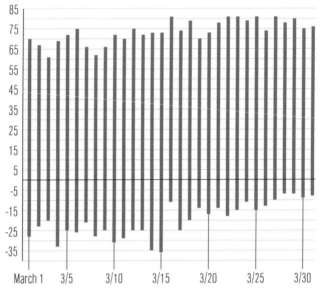

Degrees in Farenheit

15. Record highs (top of the vertical bar) and record lows (bottom of the vertical bars) for Bismarck, North Dakota. Graphed by Katie Nieland with information from the High Plains Regional Climate Center.

Figure 15 shows that record highs in Bismarck, North Dakota, during March, can exceed 80°, and record lows in the same month can fall to below -35°, which is a range of over 115 degrees.

Here are some examples of the most extreme daily ranges during March on the Great Plains:

Bismarck, North Dakota: 1874–2017

March 15: record high 73°; record low -36°; range of 109 degrees

Aberdeen, South Dakota: 1893–2017

March 15: record high 79°; record low -29°; range of 108 degrees

Lincoln, Nebraska: 1887–2017.

March 11: record high 84°; record low -19°; range of 103 degrees

Goodland, Kansas: 1895–2017

March 20: record high 90°; record low -17°; range of 107 degrees

Amarillo, Texas: 1892–2017

March 11: record high 92°; record low-3°; range of 95 degrees

Imagine for a moment that you live and work on the Great Plains and you have a job opening. After looking through all of the résumés of the applicants, you decide to bring in a candidate from San Diego, California (where they have lived their whole life) for an interview during the month of March. When you call the person in early February and invite them to come out for an interview in March, they sound excited about the opportunity. But then they ask you, "What kind of weather might I expect during the visit?" It is too far ahead to give them a detailed weather forecast so you would be stuck with describing the March climatology. You calmly tell the person, "Weather is extreme and quite variable out here on the plains during March, it could be as hot as the 90s or as cold as -20° and springtime blizzards or spring thunderstorms and tornadoes are always possible." Unless the job candidate is way into loving weather extremes, you might just hear them say, "No thanks. I think I will pass on coming in for the interview." Me, well, that's why I moved to the Great Plains!

Living on the Great Plains, for several decades, I have often witnessed this extreme variation in weather across the region. It is not uncommon in spring, during the transition between winter and summer, and in fall during the transition between summer and winter, to see dramatic contrasts within the same

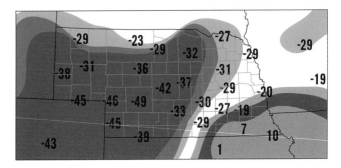

16. The twenty-four-hour temperature change from 4:00 p.m. March 22 to 4:00 p.m. March 23, 2016, as a cold front swept across Nebraska. Created by Katie Nieland with information from Rusty Dawkins, KOLN/KGIN-TV Lincoln.

state. I have seen tornado watches and severe thunderstorm warnings on the eastern end of Kansas and Nebraska and, at the same time, blizzard warnings in the western portion of these states. Many unsuspecting motorists find themselves in trouble as they transit westward from mild weather into bitter-cold blizzard conditions with highways becoming impassable.

A dramatic illustration of the extremes on the plains took place on March 23, 2016, when a strong cold front plunged south through the Great Plains with rapidly falling temperatures (see figure 16). Springtime tornado-producing thunderstorms were being replaced by winter weather conditions.

It is important to note that these dramatic and rapid extreme changes in weather on the plains often don't occur just once during a month but can be repeated over and over in the same month.

During March 2016 there were four dramatic extreme changes in the weather in North Platte, Nebraska. On March 5 the temperature was a bitter-cold 18°, but the temperature soared to 71° on that same day and to 77° the following day. On March 20,

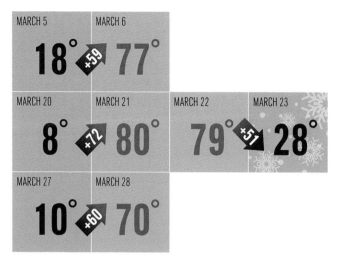

17. North Platte, Nebraska, climate data, March 2016. Created by Katie Nieland with information from the High Plains Regional Climate Center.

2016, the temperature was a midwinter cold 8° but the next day, March 21, yielded a midsummer warmth of 80°. The following day, March 22, was almost as warm at 79°, but then winter cold and snow (4.3 inches) followed that on the next day, March 23, 2016. This Great Plains temperature roller coaster contin-ued a few days later with 10° on March 27, 2016, followed by temperatures rebounding to 70° the next day, on March 28.

CHAPTER TWO

Thunderstorms and Lightning on the Great Plains

Thunderstorms are a common weather phenomenon on the Great Plains and can be dramatic and frightening or awe-inspiring, with impressive cloud structure, a lightning display reminiscent of a July Fourth fireworks display, and a beautiful rainbow to signal the end of the storm. Knowing more about how thunderstorms develop and the nature of lightning can ease the anxiety anyone might experience living in or traveling through the plains.

Climatologists estimate that, at any given moment, some 1,800 thunderstorms are in progress over the Earth's surface, with approximately 40,000 thunderstorms happening per day around the world. An estimated eighteen million thunderstorms occur each year worldwide. Among these, it is estimated that approximately 100,000 to 125,000 thunderstorms occur in the United States each year. Of that total, 10 to 20 percent of them become strong enough to be classified as "severe" And only about 1,000 (1 percent) of the 100,000-plus thunderstorms produce tornadoes. The National Weather Service (NWS) considers a thunderstorm severe if it produces hail at least one inch in diameter, winds of 58 mph or stronger, or a tornado.

How Thunderstorms Develop

Thunderstorms are generated by thermal instability in the atmosphere and represent a violent example of what scientists term "convection." Convection is the vertical circulation produced by a warm surface and it is the mechanism that gets air near the surface to rise high enough to create clouds and eventually thunderstorms. The warm air is less dense than its surroundings and—just like the smoke above the hot, less dense air over a campfire—it rises. The rising air cools along the way but remains warmer than its surroundings. Eventually the rising air cools enough that condensation takes place in the form of water droplets and a cloud. The release of a helium-filled balloon provides an example of how convection takes place. The contents of the balloon are less dense than the surroundings and it will rise up into the sky. Whereas an example of atmospheric condensation can be seen when you have a cold drink and the surrounding warm air begins to cool enough that condensation moisture begins to appear on the outside of the drinking container. The hotter the Earth's surface, the greater the difference in pressure for the rising air, and the faster the air will rise. No wonder, then, that there is so much summertime convection out here on the sunny, hot Great Plains.

Clouds are parcels of air that have been lifted high enough to condense the water vapor they contain into very small, visible particles. These particles are too small and light to fall out as rain. As the lifting process continues, these particles grow in size by collision and coalescence (colliding and merging) until they are large enough to fall against the updrafts associated with any developing convective clouds. Cumulus clouds (the puffy-looking clouds) begin their towering movement in response to atmospheric instability and convection. Warmer and lighter than the surrounding air, they rise rapidly around a strong, central updraft. These clouds expand and grow vertically, appearing as rising mounds, domes, or towers.

Although thunderstorms occur in all months of the year, it is usually not until March that severe thunderstorms return

18. Months of maximum frequency of thunderstorms across the Great Plains. Map created by Dee Ebbeka with information from the National Weather Service, Hydrometeorological Sector.

to the Great Plains. The peak occurrence of thunderstorms moves northward, along with the advancing spring warm-up, so that thunderstorm frequency peaks for much of Texas and Oklahoma in May, for eastern Kansas and eastern Nebraska in June, and the northern Great Plains (South Dakota and North Dakota on into the Canadian Prairies) peaks in July. A small

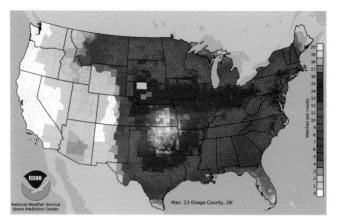

19. Map showing the average number of severe thunderstorm watches per year, 1993–2012. The frequency of severe thunderstorm watches can serve as a useful proxy for the total number of severe storms. Map courtesy of the NOAA/NWS Storm Prediction Center.

area just outside the Great Plains in northern Minnesota peaks in August. The peak frequency in September in far southeastern Texas is related to the occurrence of hurricanes that can occur in the Gulf of Mexico that time of year.

With the seasonal delay in thunderstorms going northward in the plains, it is not surprising then to see that the annual number of days with thunderstorms also decreases going from southeast Texas (sixty-plus days) to Montana–North Dakota (less than thirty days). Southwest and western Texas are semiarid regions resulting in fewer thunderstorm days there compared with most of the Great Plains region.

This unique characteristic of Great Plains thunderstorms becomes obvious in a twenty-year study conducted by the National Weather Service's Storm Prediction Center. They found that the greatest number of severe thunderstorm watches occurred on the Great Plains with the greatest frequency in the mid-plains region of Kansas and Oklahoma (as shown in figure 19). Using these data as a proxy, it also indicates that the Great Plains has the greatest number of severe thunderstorms in the U.S.

What Time of Year Are Thunderstorms Normally the Most Severe?

I often tell my students about the "front door principle" in helping them to understand the development of thunderstorms. When you open the front door of your house and it is much colder or much hotter outside, there is a sudden exchange of air into and out of the house trying to equalize the temperature differences. The larger the temperature difference, the stronger the exchange of air between the inside and outside of the house. A hot oven also illustrates the same principle. When you open the door of the oven to take out those freshly baked cookies, the hot air rushes out and slams into your face. We can likewise see this concept taking place in the atmosphere and it is called the "clash of the seasons." Early season thunderstorms feed on the "clash of the seasons" with ample supplies of lingering, cold winter air to the north and early-summer, hot and humid air off to the south. As the north-south temperature contrast diminishes, moving into summer on the Great Plains, there is less atmospheric energy to produce the severe weather associated with the thunderstorms. This means that the spring thunderstorms are much more dangerous and more severe than the summer thunderstorms on the Great Plains.

The primary mechanism responsible for thunderstorms on the plains also changes from early spring into midsummer. Springtime thunderstorms are mostly occurring as the result of strong frontal systems passing through the Great Plains, which have no real preference for time of day of occurrence. As the frontal activity diminishes to almost nonexistent by midsummer, thunderstorms are now driven by daily heating (convection) on the plains. Summer thunderstorms peak in occurrence in late afternoon, which is the usual time for the maximum daily surface temperatures.

This timing of thunderstorms plays a major role in the related daily timing of hail and tornado risk on the Great Plains, as will be noted later. Since the summer convectively driven thunderstorms are tied to the daily heating taking place on the Great Plains, summer thunderstorms typically begin to diminish rapidly in intensity during the cooler evening hours and often die off before midnight. On many a summer evening, residents on the Great Plains have seen thunderstorms off in the distance headed their way at sunset and they are hoping that these storms will bring welcome and needed rains. However, these storms can rapidly dissipate before ever reaching them.

A secondary mechanism for summertime thunderstorms on the plains is "orographic" initiation along the Front Range of the Rocky Mountains. Orographic lifting refers to air rising up the side of a mountain. Most summer mornings on the high plains are bathed in sunlight with bright blue skies. During the day, once the heating on the slopes of the Rocky Mountains gets strong enough, the rising air along the sides of the mountains begins to condense into clouds that gather at the peaks of the mountains. Moisture is scarce in the semiarid location just to the east of the Rocky Mountains so these clouds struggle to stay alive. By mid- to late afternoon, enough moisture has been gathered and the clouds begin to explode into thunderstorms. Many residents along the Front Range have told me that they can set their clocks based on the timing of these afternoon summer thunderstorms, which occur almost every day at the same time.

Sometimes these thunderstorms can remain relatively stationary and they have created devastating flash floods in the mountains that have exited out into Colorado Front Range communities like Boulder and Fort Collins, becoming deadly. Typically these orographic thunderstorms will then begin to move off of the mountain range by midafternoon and slide out onto the plains as isolated storms. They usually die off after sunset since their energy source, daytime heating and convective heating, dies off rapidly toward sunset. What is so interesting about these thunderstorms that form along the Front Range of the Rocky Mountains is that they, on rare occasion, can continue on well into the night, moving across Nebraska and Kansas and reaching, in much diminished intensity, the Missouri River valley toward dawn. This is the major exception to the diurnal rhythm in the thunderstorm cycle during summer on the Great Plains.

When Thunderstorms Go "Bad"

Typically, by midnight, the Great Plains thunderstorms have greatly weakened, lightning has ended, the winds have died down, and the thunderstorms have rained themselves out. Radar images that once showed areas of intense rainfall are now eerily quiet with absolutely no rainfall showing at all in the radar images. The sky is now filled with stars across the Great Plains and, depending on the time of the month, a moon is now shining down on the prairies. However, on rare occasions, it is instead a story of "thunderstorms gone bad." As sunset nears, these thunderstorms, instead of beginning to die off, begin to group together like an angry mob. They no longer need convection and surface heating for their survival, but instead create a self-sustaining environment that allows them to grow in strength and survive throughout the night and well into daytime. As the thunderstorms gather together, they slam air to the surface with their heavy rain and the air nearby responds by trying to balance this downward motion with rapidly ascending air, intensifying the thunderstorms.

These giant clusters of thunderstorms merge completely together and begin to function as a single megastorm known as a mesoscale convective complex, or MCC. These systems can be as much as one hundred times larger than individual thunderstorms and can spread out over areas as large as forty thousand square miles. To put this into perspective, forty thousand square miles is about half the area of South Dakota, or Kansas. The initial stage of an MCC can contain a significant amount of severe weather, but their characteristic feature is that severe weather declines and the system becomes primarily a major heavy rain producer over a large area. They commonly produce widespread rains of more than two inches and if they move slowly they can also produce flash flooding. MCC systems usually last for twelve hours or more and sometimes regenerate in the heat of the following afternoon as they move east and south across the United States.

I have seen these systems develop on the northern plains in July and August and push all the way to the Gulf States twenty-four hours later. Compared to typical hit-or-miss afternoon convective thunderstorms in the Great Plains, these "bad thunderstorms" can actually bring widespread rains that can benefit agriculture. I have often heard farmers happily call these "million-dollar rains," after a beneficial MCC passes over the region during a dry spell. However, it is possible to have too much of a good thing, as occurred during the summer of 1993. Extensive flooding in the eastern Great Plains and Lower Midwest in the summer of 1993 resulted largely from the more than forty MCCs that had amassed over the region, far exceeding the average of twelve for a typical summer. This flooding affected drainage basins in Iowa, Nebraska, Illinois, and Missouri and caused $20 billion in damages, making it the costliest flood in U.S. history.

Lightning

The stage is set for lightning when warm moist air in vapor form rises into the cooler air aloft and begins to condense into water droplets, creating cumulus clouds. The change in state from vapor to liquid releases heat energy, termed the "latent heat of condensation," and this helps drive these clouds even higher into the atmosphere. Cumulus clouds are initially dominated by upward vertical motion, but eventually rain begins to fall, dragging air with it back down toward the Earth's surface resulting in both ascending and descending air currents within the same cloud. With precipitation falling from the cumulus cloud, it is now termed a "cumulonimbus" cloud (*nimbus* is Latin for "rain bearing").

The normal electrical distribution in the atmosphere prior to thunderstorm formation is a slight positive electrical charge, with the Earth's surface having a slight negative electrical charge. However, things are about to change dramatically as turbulence continues to increase and huge amounts of condensation heat are released into the cloud, pushing the cloud higher and higher into the atmosphere and well above the freezing level. Cumulonimbus clouds on the Great Plains can reach elevations as high as sixty-five thousand feet above sea level, which is twice the typical height of a transcontinental jet aircraft in midflight. The ice crystals in the upper portion of the cumulonimbus cloud typically take on a positive charge and the water droplets are generally negative in the bottom portion of the cloud.

I wish we could see what happens next with our eyes, but we can't. The ground cannot remain negatively charged with the bottom area of the cloud also negatively charged. Why not? A magnet is the best example. A magnet will attract an object of the opposite charge but repel, push away, objects of the same charge. If the ground did not switch its charge from negative to positive, the bottom of the cloud with its negative charge would be repelled by the negative charge of the Earth's surface and the cloud would shoot up into the sky. I actually think that would be fun to watch if this would happen, but instead a positive charge is induced at the Earth's surface directly beneath the developing storm cloud.

Things are really twisted now. The Earth's surface has switched its polarity from negative to positive beneath the cloud and there are regions of positive and negative charges growing in intensity within the cloud. This imbalance of electrical charge eventually erupts into electrical discharges between the oppositely charged regions within the cloud, between nearby clouds, and between the cloud and the ground. This is nature attempting to restore order within the atmosphere. This energy heats the air in the channel to above 50,000° in only a few millionths of a second. The air that is now heated to such a high temperature has had no time to expand, so it is now at a very high pressure. This high-pressure air along the lightning channel then explodes outward into the surrounding air and becomes an ordinary sound wave, producing thunder. This transition from a small puffy cumulus cloud to a turbulent, electrified thunderstorm can occur in as little as thirty minutes.

Over the contiguous forty-eight states, an average of twenty million cloud-to-ground flashes have been detected every year since the lightning detection network covered all of the continental United States, in 1989. In addition, about half of all flashes have more than one ground strike point, so at least thirty million points on the ground are struck on the average each year in the U.S. There are roughly five to ten times more lightning flashes within and between clouds than actually reach the ground.

And, as an interesting side note, lightning sometimes is actually initiated from the ground up to the cloud. If you shuffle your feet across a carpeted floor you might have experienced a small static buildup and a spark comes from your fingers when you touch something metal. You can actually hear the static discharges when you take off a woolen sweater. Socks sticking together with static charge when they come out of the clothes dryer is an example of building up electrical charge. The air flowing and encountering friction as it moves along the surface of the land can also pick up static charge and initiate an electrical release upward toward the thunderstorm cloud. This is difficult to see with the naked eye. This upward stroke also happens so fast (in about one-millionth of a second) that the human eye doesn't see the actual formation of the upward stroke. Once the connection is made, the massive amount of charge in the cloud comes surging down toward the Earth's surface in a noticeable cloud-to-ground lightning strike.

Some Lightning Safety Advice for Surviving Storms on the Great Plains

It is useful to know that you can calculate the distance between your location and the lightning. Count the number of seconds between the flash of lightning and the sound of thunder. The delay between when you see lightning and when you hear thunder occurs because sound travels much more slowly than light. Sound travels one mile every five seconds, so divide the number of seconds by five to determine how many miles away the lightning occurred. Thunder can be heard from a maximum distance of about fifteen miles under good atmospheric conditions. Even though sound from lightning strikes can't be heard very far away, it is possible to see lightning in the distance on the Great Plains from over 150 miles away. On several occasions on warm summer nights, I have seen lightning in the distance, checked the current radar online, and found that, although I am in Lincoln, Nebraska, the storms have been as far away as St. Joseph, Missouri, Columbus, Nebraska, and Sioux City, Iowa.

20. Lightning strikes a tree. Note the upward surge of electricity just to the left of the main lightning channel, which is the initiation of lightning from the near surface up to the cloud. Courtesy of NOAA.

Although many people assume it must be raining where lightning is going to strike, that is not the case. Lightning can come out the side of a thunderstorm and strike a location miles away from the storm where the sun is shining. "Bolts from the blue" can strike ten to fifteen miles from the thunderstorm, which means that if you can hear thunder you are at risk and should seek shelter. If you are caught outside with no safe shelter anywhere nearby, the following actions may reduce your risk: immediately get off elevated areas such as hills, mountain ridges, or peaks; never shelter under an isolated tree (see figure 20 for a dramatic photo of lightning striking a tree); never use a cliff

LOCATION	2016 TOTAL	2007 - 2016 AVG.	STRIKES PER SQ. MILE
North Dakota	612,619	326,292	4.6
South Dakota	716,916	508,125	6.6
Nebraska	826,613	773,204	9.4
Kansas	1,278,681	1,059,261	12.9
Oklahoma	1,328,138	1,117,379	16.0
Texas	4,066,432	2,992,944	11.3

21. Cloud-to-ground lightning strikes. Table created by Alexa Horn with information from http://www.lightningsafety.noaa.gov/stats /07–16_Flash_Density_State.pdf and from the Vaisala National Lightning Data Network.

or rocky overhang for shelter; immediately get out and away from ponds, lakes, and other bodies of water; and, stay away from objects that conduct electricity (barbed wire fences, power lines, windmills, etc.). Never lie flat on the ground to avoid being struck by lightning. Lightning electrical surge can spread out sixty feet after striking the ground, so lying flat increases your chance of being affected by potentially deadly ground current (see figure 21 for a frequency summary of cloud-to-ground lightning strikes across five Great Plains states). If you are caught outside in a thunderstorm, you need to keep moving toward a safe shelter. Cars are safe shelter and, ironically, it is not the rubber tires that keep you safe, it is the metal shell that deflects the lightning around the car and into the ground. Find additional safety information at: http://www.lightningsafety .noaa.gov/.

CHAPTER THREE

Hail-Producing Storms on the Great Plains

Most people are familiar with the attribution of "Tornado Alley" to the Great Plains region (more about Tornado Alley later in chapter 6), but the Great Plains is also home to what can be called "Hail Alley."

Hailstorm Climatology

Figure 22 shows us hail events mapped across the United States for the year 2017. This mapping of hail damage reports is in fact typical of every year and clearly shows the greatest frequency taking place on the Great Plains from Texas to North Dakota.

Florida has more thunderstorms than does the Great Plains, but the air is so humid there that thunderstorms in that region don't need to build very high before they start dumping their copious amounts of moisture. Because Florida thunderstorms don't rise very far into subfreezing air, the probability of hail occurrences is significantly reduced. Thunderstorms on the Great Plains, however, occur in an environment of limited atmospheric moisture and can grow as high as sixty-five thousand feet, well above the typical freezing level of around fifteen thousand feet on the Great Plains during the summer.

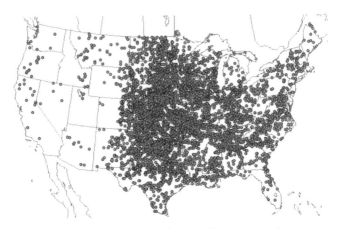

22. Map depicting hail reports in the United States, 2017. Courtesy of the NOAA/NWS Storm Prediction Center, http://www.spc.noaa.gov/climo/online/monthly/2017_annual_summary.html.

Large hailstones in the Great Plains can develop layers of ice, like an onion, if they travel up and down between the freezing and above-freezing regions of a thunderstorm. One can tell how many times a hailstone has traveled to the top of the storm by counting the layers of ice. Large hail can also have few or no layers if they are "balanced" in an updraft. On occasion, hailstones will start to melt within a cloud, then slam together in the cloud becoming a large composite and very irregularly shaped hailstone. Hail falls to the ground when the thunderstorm's updraft can no longer support the weight of the ice or if the updraft weakens.

Hail can sometimes contain foreign matter, such as pebbles, leaves, twigs, nuts, and insects. The stronger the updraft, the larger the hailstone can grow. It is here on the Great Plains where we find thunderstorms with some of the strongest updrafts. According to NOAA, large hailstones out here on the Great Plains can fall at speeds faster than 100 miles (or 160 kilometers) per hour. The

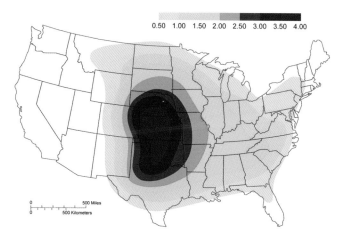

23. Map showing the average number of days with hail 1.25 inches or larger. Hail which is 1.25 inches or larger (size of a ping-pong ball) is large enough to cause damage to exposed surfaces. Map created by the author with information from the NOAA/NWS Storm Prediction Center.

large size and speed of hailstones on the Great Plains can also be life threatening. A child was killed in Fort Collins, Colorado, in 1979 when struck in the head by a large hailstone. In Lake Worth Village, Texas, on March 28, 2000, a nineteen-year-old man was struck by softball-sized hail while trying to move a new car. He died the following day from associated head injuries. Livestock fatalities from hail are also fairly common.

The Great Plains, Home to the Largest Hail in the United States

The frequency of hail measuring 1.25 inches or greater is the highest in the Great Plains, with the highest frequency extending from south-central Nebraska through central Oklahoma (see these data mapped in figure 23). The frequency of hail 2.0 inches or greater is also the highest in the Great Plains, with the greatest frequency in central Oklahoma into north-central Texas.

The Seasonality of Hailstorms

Similar to the frequency of thunderstorms, the hail season peaks earlier in the southern portion of the Great Plains and later in the northern plains. In mid-April the greatest probability of hail occurrence is centered in Oklahoma and northeast Texas. The highest probability of hail across the greater United States is in mid-May, and the area of greatest frequency has expanded northward into south-central Kansas. By mid-June the probability of hail has diminished only slightly but the area of highest frequency has continued to move northward and is now in western Kansas and southwest Nebraska. The probability of hail in the Great Plains rapidly decreases going into July and August, and the highest probabilities have moved out of the southern Great Plains into the central and northern Great Plains. It is an unfortunate coincidence that the peak harvesting of winter wheat on the Great Plains moves northward at the same time that the time of peak hail occurrence is moving across the same region. Many a farmer has lost their entire wheat crop to the scourge of the spring and early summertime hail on the plains.

Hail and the Early Wagon Train Emigrants of the Nineteenth Century

Dr. Merlin Lawson, professor emeritus at the University of Nebraska–Lincoln, in his publication *The Climate of the Great American Desert*, used military fort data as well as historical letters and diaries of the emigrants who traveled across the Great Plains to reconstruct the climate of the Great Plains at the time of their passage. These historical documents also describe extreme weather events including tornadoes, floods, and hailstorms. As he noted in this publication, "The brilliant lightning storms, high winds, and hail of gross proportions amazed and intimidated those unaccustomed to such violence from the heavens." Almost everyone probably knows the comment that Dorothy made in the movie *The Wizard of Oz* when she exclaimed, "My goodness Toto, I don't think we are in Kansas anymore." I imagine that these pioneers, coming from temperate European climates and crossing the Great Plains—enduring weather extremes like they had never seen before—must have proclaimed like Dorothy did, "My goodness, I don't think we are in Europe anymore."

Lawson noted that, on average, the diarists recorded two hailstorms during their crossing of the Great Plains. All of these hailstorms were located west of Grand Island, Nebraska, where the main trail met the Platte River. Lawson notes, "It appears that near Ash Hollow, the very first emigrants along the trail were unfortunate enough to experience the most devastating hailstorm imaginable." In *The Climate of the Great American Desert*, Lawson cites William Johnston, who passed the region of the storm five days later, noting that it had wreaked havoc on a wagon train, and he described what they had encountered:

> A number of emigrant trains were passed, among them one called, the Platte City Company, commanded by Colonel Ransom; from whom we learned of a hailstorm of considerable violence, encountered on Tuesday last, ten or twelve miles west of Ash Hollow. Their wagon covers and tents had been riddled by hail stones, some of which were of extraordinary size, weighing as much as eight and nine ounces each. The cattle of some emigrant parties were so badly frightened that they ran in various directions for many miles from their owner. When passing the locality where this occurred, we had noticed the ground was torn up, and in places forming

large cavities, but were unable to conjecture the cause until learning these facts. We are also able to account for the cold weather which followed. The storm we had experienced in the evening referred to, had not been accompanied by hail.

Lawson relates another devastating hailstorm encountered by these emigrants: "Another hailstorm along the South Platte proved as vicious. In a letter later published in the *Detroit Daily Advertiser* James Lyon wrote: 'all the wagon's covers looked as if they had received a shower of brickbats: and the men one would have thought had received a shower of Indian arrows, to have seen the blood streaming from their heads . . . but none of them had any fracture of the skull.'"

The Economic Impact of Hailstorms on the Plains

One of the costliest hailstorms on the plains occurred on its western margin when the Denver, Colorado, area, on July 11, 1990, took a direct hit by a prolific hail-making thunderstorm. When it was all over, damage totals close to $600 million were reported, which was the greatest property loss from hail ever reported from one storm up to that time. However, this record amount of property loss by hail was soon eclipsed by a May 5, 1995, Fort Worth, Texas, hailstorm that set the new record for costliest property damage at an estimated $1.1 billion in damages. If adjusted for inflation, that 1995 storm in 2017 dollars would be more than $1.6 billion in damages.

But wait, there's more! Along comes spring 2016 with four hailstorms in three weeks' time in northern Texas, resulting in an astounding total of $3 billion in hail damages. The National Weather Service in Austin and San Antonio, Texas, provides the following totals:

March 17, 2016: Fort Worth area—$600 million

March 23, 2016: Wylie—$700 million

April 11, 2016: Plano—$300 million

April 12, 2016: Amarillo (Bexar County)—$1.4 billion

The April 12, 2016, Amarillo hailstorm, which produced almost $1.4 billion in estimated insured losses, was the costliest hailstorm in U.S. history to that point. Insured losses to automobiles from the April 12 storm reached $560 million, while damage to homes approached $800 million, according to the insurance trade association. More than 110,000 vehicles were damaged, and thousands of homes suffered roof damage.

The insurance industry, providing both crop insurance and household insurance (home and auto), has to deal with numerous damage claims each year on the plains. Looking at just one year (2015) and only one insurance company (State Farm Insurance), the following is a listing of the number of hail-damage claims filed in several of the Great Plains states.

Texas: 51,193 hail-damage claims

Colorado: 42,365 hail-damage claims

Kansas: 11,562 hail-damage claims

Nebraska: 21,326 hail-damage claims

South Dakota: 12,367 hail-damage claims

In two neighboring states, Missouri counted 23,019 hail-damage claims and Iowa checked in with 12,367 hail-damage claims.

Looking at the next year, 2016, with data also provided by State Farm Insurance, Nebraska was in the top five states in the nation for most hail claims. Here is the press release provided by Jim Camoriano of State Farm Insurance.

STATE FARM—April 1, 2017—The Cornhusker State is back in the Top 5 in the nation with the most State Farm hail claims.

RANK	STATE	COST ($)
1	TEXAS	145,000
2	COLORADO	34,900
3	MISSOURI	27,700
4	ILLINOIS	24,500
5	NEBRASKA	17,500
6	ARKANSAS	14,500
7	KANSAS	12,600
8	OKLAHOMA	11,000
9	INDIANA	10,000
10	LOUISIANA	9,100

24. Hail-damage costs ranked by state. Table created by Alexa Horn with information from State Farm Insurance.

In 2016, the insurer paid out on 17,500 vehicle and homeowners hail claims in Nebraska, nearly three times as many as the year before. Almost all of those claims came from dual storms that pummeled Lincoln and Omaha the first week in May.

"That pair of hailstorms generated more than $172 million in State Farm claim payments across the state," said Jim

25. I conducted a live report with KETV Omaha from my hail-battered neighborhood. Photo courtesy of the author.

Camoriano, State Farm spokesman. "It's a reminder that severe weather is a substantial and standard part of our lives. Property owners can take steps now to minimize damage from future storms."

Nebraska was also number five two years ago, in 2014. The next year the state fell to thirteenth in the country with fewer than sixteen claims, before grabbing the fifth spot again.

Damage caused by hail cost State Farm policyholders across the United States more than $3 billion in 2016. Our top ten states in 2016 with the most paid hail claims are shown by the table in figure 24.

I had experienced many hail occurrences while living in Nebraska and traveling throughout the Great Plains, but nothing comes close to what happened to me on May 9, 2016. The hail storm lasted for an hour, never slowing down. Although much of the hail was small, there were hailstones as large as tennis balls and softballs falling in my neighborhood (see figure 25).

26. Hail damage on the roof of a neighbor's home. Photo by Bill Sorensen.

Some of these larger hailstones actually went through the roofs in my neighborhood.

My neighbor, Bill Sorensen, who lives across the street from me, posted this on Facebook: "I found the source of the leak. What does it take to bust a 1.5-inch hole straight through asphalt shingles and wooden roof beams?" Note the photo documentation of this damage in figure 26.

As the storm began, I started to give updates on several social media platforms and I continued to give live coverage of the storm from my house during the entire hailstorm. Many of these posts began to show up on local T V stations here in Lincoln and in Omaha as well as on social media platforms for radio and newspapers.

According to Twitter Analytics (a program that keeps track of the activity at a Twitter website), the above "tweet" posting alone was seen by 42,497 people and retweeted 6,104 times. The two-day May 9–10, 2016, Twitter Analytics summary had a total of 148,500 views of the Twitter postings that I made during the hailstorm and the next day as I surveyed the damage. Figure 27 shows us measuring one of the hailstones that fell into our yard from that storm.

The Records for Largest Hail on the Plains

It is difficult to create a climatology of the largest observed hailstones. Many hailstones that are large will break apart when hitting structures or the hard ground. It is interesting to note that the largest hailstones are in fact not a single hailstone but are the result of many smaller hailstones being fused together while traveling throughout the severe thunderstorm. Every once in a while a very large hailstone will land on a soft-enough surface so that it remains intact and can be recovered and quickly put into a freezer. Here are the known top four largest hailstones that were recovered and measured in the U.S.

27. Measuring a hailstone that fell into my yard on May 9, 2016. Photo by the author.

1. Vivian, South Dakota, on June 23, 2010, with a diameter of 8 inches and a circumference of 18.6 inches.
2. Aurora, Nebraska, on June 22, 2003, with a diameter of 7 inches and a circumference of 18.75 inches.
3. Coffeyville, Kansas, on September 3, 1970, with a diameter of 5.7 inches and a circumference of 17.5 inches.
4. Potter, Nebraska, on July 6, 1928, with a diameter of around 7 inches (and unknown circumference).

The National Climate Extremes Committee, (a part of the National Oceanic and Atmospheric Administration) is responsible for validating national records such as these. They were able to personally examine the Aurora hailstone of June 2003 and brought it to the National Center for Atmospheric Research in Boulder, Colorado, where it will be preserved indefinitely. The Aurora hailstone, although ranked second largest in diameter, is still ranked the largest for hailstone circumference. You can

28. A car badly damaged from a hailstorm in Weatherford, Oklahoma, on July 1, 1940. Courtesy of the U.S. Weather Bureau.

investigate information such as this on the NOAA website at https://www.ncdc.noaa.gov/monitoring-content/extremes /ncec/vivian-hailstone-final.pdf; https://www.weather.gov/gid /jun-22-2003 megastorm.

The NOAA photo library has some historical hail-damage photos dating back to the 1920s from Texas. Automobiles were built out of steel back then with no plastic bumpers and no thin aluminum outer bodies. The photo in figure 28 shows the impressive destruction of one of these automobiles by hail.

CHAPTER FOUR

Snowstorms and Ice Storms

It snows every winter across much of the United States. However, the unique physical geography and climate of the Great Plains can result in historic blizzards and ice storms for this region. A blizzard is a storm with sustained winds in excess of 35 miles per hour, temperatures below 20°, and blowing or falling snow that reduces visibility to less than a quarter mile. The English word *blizzard* originated in the northern plains during the mid-nineteenth century, perhaps derived from the German *blitzkrieg*, meaning lightning-like, which accurately portrays the power and swiftness of Great Plains blizzards. It should be remembered that a heavy snowfall is not a blizzard, and in fact blizzards can occur with only light snowfall. It is the high winds and reduced visibility from blowing snow along with bitter-cold temperatures that define a blizzard occurrence.

Although most common in winter, Great Plains blizzards also occur in autumn and spring. The meteorological stage is set when a mass of cold polar air moves rapidly southward from higher latitudes and encounters a strong northward flow of moist, tropical air from lower latitudes. When a low-pressure cell encounters the energy difference between these two unlike air masses, it rapidly grows in strength, becoming a "deepening low." As the low-pressure cell strengthens, it feeds itself by pulling southward even greater amounts of cold air and northward even larger amounts of warm air and moisture. By the time the blizzard reaches full intensity, it is not unusual to have severe thunderstorms and tornadoes across the southern portion of this major storm. Wind-chill temperatures often drop to life-threatening levels across the northern portion of the storm. The winds pack the snow, making it extremely difficult to walk through and to remove from driveways and sidewalks. Although urban highways are usually opened within a day or so of a blizzard, rural roads often remain impassible for many days. Blizzards, on rare occasion, have occurred as far south as northern Texas, but they increase in frequency northward up the Great Plains. Nebraska, for example, averages one to two blizzards per year, while the southern parts of the Prairie Provinces, Canada, average from three to five blizzards per year. Some of these blizzards are historically noteworthy.

"School Children's Storm," January 12, 1888

The tales of some of the Great Plains blizzards rise to legendary status, and the blizzard of January 12, 1888, is one of them. It impacted the region from Texas to Alberta. The suddenness of the blizzard conditions resulted in 235 fatalities as a result of this storm as the victims traveled even short distances. The blizzard hit the central plains when schools were dismissing the students for the day, and some teachers allowed their children to walk home in the hope that they could get home before the arriving storm increased in intensity. Other teachers released their students early, hoping they would arrive home before its full fury. But this was not meant to be. Temperatures quickly plummeted to nearly 40 below zero, and 60-mile-per-hour winds with snow as fine as sifted flour reduced visibility to practically zero on the open prairie. It is significant to note that at this time in history, there would not have been any paved roads, street lights, or any structures that would have helped guide them toward home. In Bon Homme County, Dakota Territory, the wind scattered a teacher and her nine students as they attempted to get to safety after leaving their schoolhouse. They all died and were not found until the snow melted months later. Parents also perished as they left the safety of their homes in an attempt to locate their children. Some details of the struggle to survive the fury of the storm are chronicled in a diary now in the Nebraska State Historical Society archives: "We could not see five feet from us in any direction. We got within twenty feet of the house, got lost, and shouted as loud as we could, but could hear nothing but threat from that fateful wind. Old Tom Keller was frozen to death that night. A man by the name Glaze was found next morning, stark and stiff within ten feet of his door."

There is a Nebraska Blizzard of 1888 Historical Marker memorializing the "school children's storm," which is located in Valley County, nine miles south of Ord, Nebraska. This historical marker records the following text:

> On January 12, 1888, a sudden fierce blizzard slashed across the Midwest. The temperature fell to between 30 and 40 degrees below zero. A howling northwest wind swept the plains. The storm raged for 12 to 18 hours and is probably the most severe single blizzard to have hit Nebraska since the settlement of the state.
>
> Sometimes called "the school children's storm," the blizzard caught many children away from home. Many acts of heroism were performed by parents, teachers, and the children themselves.
>
> The story of Minnie Freeman has become symbolic of these many acts of heroism. Miss Freeman, still in her teens at the time, was teaching at school near here. When the wind tore the roof off the sod school schoolhouse, Miss Freeman

saved her pupils by leading them through the storm to a farmhouse a half mile away.

Many other teachers performed similar acts of heroism, and at least one lost her life in the attempt. No accurate count of the total deaths from the storm is possible, but estimates for Nebraska have ranged from 40 to 100.

This storm impacted popular culture. The "Song of the Great Blizzard 1888: Thirteen Were Saved" (figure 29) commemorates Miss Minnie Freeman, the schoolteacher who exhibited great bravery and saved the lives of her thirteen students during the blizzard of 1888.

David Laskin's book, *The Children's Blizzard*, which focuses on the blizzard of 1888, describes the long-term impact of the blizzard: "Thousands of impoverished Northern European immigrants were promised that the prairie offered land, freedom, and hope. The disastrous blizzard of 1888 revealed that their free homestead was not a paradise but a hard, unforgiving place governed by natural forces they neither understood nor controlled, and America's heartland would never be the same."

The Blizzard Voices, by Ted Kooser, is a collection of poems recording the devastation unleashed on the Great Plains by the 1888 blizzard. *The Blizzard Voices* is based on the actual reminiscences of the survivors as recorded in documents from the time and written reminiscences from years later. As described by the publisher: "Here are the haunting voices of the men and women who were teaching school, working the land, and tending the house when the storm arrived and changed their lives forever."

Pleasant Hill School Bus Blizzard Tragedy, March 26, 1931

The Pleasant Hill School was located in Kiowa County, Colorado, less than two miles from the Kansas border, and consisted

29. "Song of the Great Blizzard 1888: Thirteen Were Saved" or "Nebraska's Fearless Maid," song and chorus by Wm. Vincent, published by Lyon & Healy, Chicago. Courtesy of the Nebraska State Historical Society.

of two one-room schoolhouses with a teacher for each building. Geographically, it was located midway between the northwest and southwest corners of Kansas. The two one-room school-houses were built in an isolated, totally rural location located fourteen miles south of the nearest settlement, Towner, Colorado. Some of the media at the time incorrectly called it the Towner school but in fact it was not in the village of Towner and the Towner school had no serious impacts from this blizzard. The students were all from farm families living in the vicinity of the school, including some students from nearby western Kansas. This area of the Great Plains was basically a gently rolling, treeless landscape and prone to strong winds any time of the year. The nearest location that would have any weather data from this time period is Goodland, Kansas (see figure 30).

The residents living out here in this very rural area had none of the benefits of today's communications, so they had no advance warning that their recent early spring mid-70° weather was going to suddenly turn into a dangerous, bitter-cold blizzard.

As the bus driver arrived at the school on the morning of Thursday, March 26, 1931, snow had already begun to fall and the winds were quickly getting stronger. The two teachers told the bus driver to turn around and take the children back home, arguing that there wasn't enough food or firewood to keep the school warm for the students to remain there for a prolonged period of time should the storm persist overnight. The bus driver was advised to seek out a nearby farmhouse if the storm prevented him from going further along on his route. It was argued that the students would be safer in a heated farmhouse and that there would be food for them there as well.

The bus driver headed out on his route into a raging plains blizzard with very strong winds beginning to drift the snow and reducing visibility to only a few feet. The roads at that time were not paved but were merely lanes through farm fields connecting

Goodland, KS, March 22-31, 1931

DATE	HIGH (°F)	LOW (°F)	PRECIP.	SNOWFALL (in.)
03/22/1931	74	35	0.00	0.0
03/23/1931	62	37	0.00	0.0
03/24/1931	50	29	0.00	0.0
03/25/1931	45	25	0.04	0.0
03/26/1931	33	-1	0.62	9.0
03/27/1931	8	-3	0.08	1.0
03/28/1931	30	3	0.00	0.0
03/29/1931	25	19	0.12	1.0
03/30/1931	27	17	0.12	0.8
03/31/1931	50	13	0.00	0.0

Precip. = precipitation total

30. Nearest precipitation data for Pleasant Hill school bus blizzard tragedy. Table created by Alexa Horn with information from the High Plains Regional Climate Center.

the various farm houses. As the authors of *Children of the Storm*, Ariana Harner and Clark Secrest, explained, "Pleasant Hill's gravel roads did not follow section lines, as they do today, and some roads weren't roads at all. Instead, residents took direct routes across the fields to get to a neighbor's house." It didn't take long before the bus ran into trouble. Lost in the storm with almost no visibility, the bus driver drove the bus into a small ditch and the bus was hopelessly stuck in the snow.

The school bus (see figure 31) was not really a bus but was a modified 1929 Chevrolet truck with a wooden school-bus body attached to its frame. The seats were wooden benches. Two of the rear windows of the bus were broken out and merely covered with cardboard. The bus did not have any heat and there was no way to communicate with anyone to seek help and to

31. Pleasant Hill school bus involved in the 1931 blizzard tragedy. Photo courtesy of Kiowa County, Colorado.

rescue the students. Parents interviewed after the storm said that when their children didn't return home, they assumed that they were safe either at the school or a nearby farmhouse.

During the afternoon, the bus driver had two of the older children leave the bus to see if there was a farmhouse where everyone could seek shelter. However, as the two students stepped away from the bus, the strong winds repeatedly knocked them over so that they had to return to the bus. As it grew dark, the blizzard maintained its full ferocity all night long. And what a horrible night it must have been for those children and the bus driver who was responsible for their safety. The storm was still raging when Friday morning (March 27) came. By now, temperatures had fallen below zero and wind speeds were estimated to be in excess of 70 mph. Despite these life-threatening conditions the bus driver felt he had no choice but to head off on foot to find help, knowing that the children would not be able to survive much longer in the unheated bus. He told the older children to look after the younger ones and he stepped outside. His frozen body was found by searchers twenty-four hours later, 3.5 miles south of the bus. Even though he was wearing gloves, his hands were badly cut from holding onto a barbed wire fence that he used to guide him along in the powerful blinding blizzard.

Shortly after the bus driver left to seek help, one of the children stopped moving and the other children realized that she had died. Over the next few hours two more children died. The older children took the three bodies and placed them together at the back of the bus. I cannot imagine how frightened the children were at this point with the only adult out in the storm and watching their classmates die and several others being close to death.

By late afternoon on Friday the storm began to quickly decrease in intensity and, as the sun began to break through the clouds, several parents went out in search of the bus, hoping to find it at a nearby farmhouse. Two parents stumbled upon the bus, broke open the door to get inside and put the students onto their farm wagon and drove them to a farmhouse only a half mile north (opposite the direction that the bus driver had gone). The schoolchildren had spent thirty-two hours on the unheated bus and several were in critical condition.

According to the report prepared in 2012 by authors Laurie Simmons and Thomas Simmons for the Kiowa County Historic Preservation, when they reached the farmhouse, the men tried to warm the children by massaging their limbs with snow and salt. It was explained that this was a common practice at that time and is clearly not something we would do today. The children were wrapped in blankets and given food. Some of the children had painfully swollen legs and several could not feel their legs. As they "thawed out," the pain, typical of frostbite, became awful. Despite being rescued, two more of the schoolchildren died later that evening.

Nothing remains at the site of the two one-room school houses, and most of the farmhouses that had children attending the Pleasant Hill School are also gone. It is hard to imagine that any good came out of this disaster, but it did. This event was the catalyst for bus safety legislation in Colorado and eventually across the United States. In 1939 a series of national standards and regulations were established for school buses including on-board communication systems and a shelter-in-place policy. It is interesting to note that the standard bright yellow that we find on school buses is meant to increase their visibility should any rescue be necessary.

Endless Snowstorms, Winter of 1948–49

A series of snowstorms impacted Colorado, Nebraska, North Dakota, South Dakota, and Wyoming starting in November 1948 and not ending until February 1949. More than 240,000 people were trapped in their rural homes during these storms. In November 1948 a severe blizzard passed over parts of Nebraska, Wyoming, and Colorado, dumping several feet of snow, blocking transportation lines, and isolating towns and ranches throughout the region. Next, the so-called bookend blizzards both occurred in January 1949. A total of up to thirty inches of snow fell across an even wider area than the November storm, with drifts up to fifty feet high. Chadron, Nebraska, had a two-day total of forty-one inches of snow, which remains the Nebraska state record for a two-day snowfall. Newspaper editors estimated that 7,500 passengers were stranded on fifty stalled trains from Illinois to Idaho. The second of the bookend blizzards occurred on January 27–28, 1949, in the eastern end of the state, with sustained winds of 50 to 60 miles per hour and dumping thirteen inches of snow on Omaha. The storm shut down Lincoln and Omaha for several days.

The National Guard responded with snow plows and M–29 cargo carriers known as Weasels, essentially enclosed jeeps with tank treads, to rescue people and provide emergency supplies. State highway departments struggled to open roads. Once President Truman declared the region a major disaster area on January 29, the Army Corp of Engineers, National Guard, U.S. Air Force, and state and local agencies officially responded with "Operation Snowbound." The air force launched "Operation Hay lift," to airdrop supplies to snowed-in families and bales of hay to starving livestock. Army Weasels ran atop the snow to bring supplies to stormbound residents. Following behind were mobile strike forces made up of bulldozers, snowplows, fuel trucks, wreckers, tractors, and cargo vehicles. At its peak, 6,237 people participated in the effort, including 807 U.S. Army officers, 959 Army Corps employees, and over 4,000 contractors. They used 1,654 pieces of snow-clearing equipment in a disaster area covering 193,000 square miles with an estimated population of 1.2 million.

The Nebraska State Historical Society has an excellent summary of the timeline for Operation Snowbound at http://www .nebraskahistory.org/publish/publicat/timeline/snowbound _48–49.htm. The report describes the rescue operations:

> Farmers used many different kinds of rigs to take groceries and other needed items home. All roads were blocked and many remained that way until spring. A local man who had been a pilot in WW 2, flew a ski-plane, taking medicine, groceries, etc., also bringing some sick people to the doctor and hospital when needed. . . . The army men came with a machine called a weasel. It could be driven over snowbanks to reach homes. Highway 81 was the only hard surfaced road into Wausa at that time, so it was possible to get supplies when the road was open. Other towns weren't as fortunate. The handcar on the railroad was used between Wausa and Bloomfield. . . . The final total of snow was 90 inches. Some snowbanks were 25 to 35 feet high.

Clearance efforts made it apparent just how intractable that much snow could become: "Several thick layers of ice in the snow banks made clearing of snow impossible in places, as snow plows couldn't move it, so dynamite was used in some places. One snowplow operator from Iowa said, 'I didn't know Nebraska had concrete in their snowbanks.'"

The Blizzard of January 10–11, 1975

This blizzard is noteworthy for its occurrence in a more modern era with advance warnings from the National Weather Service. This blizzard was a "textbook" storm, developing from a low-pressure system that dropped out of Colorado into Oklahoma and then headed north to Minnesota. The storm's counter-clockwise wind flow dragged down Arctic air from Canada and pulled up tropical moisture from the Gulf of Mexico (see the storm's time frame and temperature plotted on the map in figure 32). The low-pressure system continued to strengthen as it moved northward, producing some all-time record low-pressure readings in the plains. The storm's intense pressure gradient resulted in near hurricane force winds that raged for two days across the eastern portion of Nebraska. The Nebraska State Patrol shut down most of the roads in the Lincoln and Omaha region. The travel impact was even worse going north into the Dakotas and especially Minnesota.

A More Recent Blizzard, October 3–5, 2013

These winter storms, filled with nature's fury, no longer appear on the plains without warning; however, their impacts can still be quite severe. This storm struck portions of North and South Dakota, Wyoming, and Nebraska.

Between October 3 and 5, 2013, an unusually early blizzard smothered northeastern Wyoming and western South Dakota with wet, heavy snow along with rain, hail, thunderstorms,

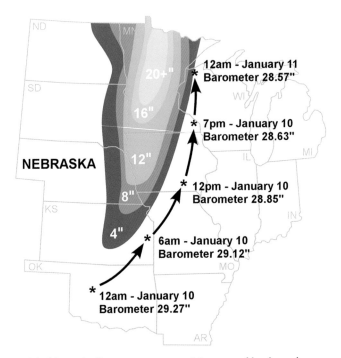

32. The blizzard of January 10–11, 1975. Map created by the author with information from National Weather Service data.

and even tornadoes. In South Dakota's Black Hills, the storm dropped more than three feet of snow in some areas (with an impressive fifty-five inches falling in Lead, South Dakota), knocking out power for about twenty-five thousand people and killing tens of thousands of cattle. The cattle, which had not yet grown the thick winter coats that allow them to survive the winters, were grazing in unprotected summer pastures when the storm hit. Many animals simply froze to death or suffocated after being soaked by freezing rain and then buried by snow. About 15 to 20 percent of South Dakota's cattle may have been killed, according to the South Dakota Growers Association.

Warmer weather and rain right after the blizzard then compli-
cated cleanup efforts, melting much of the snow and leaving
farms coated with so much mud that fields and roads were
impassable for days. The direct economic loss was estimated
to exceed $40 million.

As is so often observed on the plains, the weather during that
blizzard varied considerably across the region, ranging from
winter conditions to springlike warmth and tornadoes. The
Storm Prediction Center data archive lists a total of eighteen
tornado reports (nine in northeast Nebraska, eight in northwest
Iowa, and one in southeast South Dakota) and thirty reports
of hail stretching from southwest Oklahoma, across the mid-
plains, and into north-central Iowa.

The Forgotten Snowstorm, May 1947

The opposite of legendary is the forgotten snowstorm of May
27–29, 1947. It is noteworthy not so much for the amounts of
snow but for how late in the spring this winter event occurred.
Trees were in full leaf across Nebraska and many farm fields
were planted. School was out for the summer, and then, winter
briefly returned to the Great Plains.

On the morning of May 27, 1947, a developing low-pressure
system was located over central Nevada. It was this low that
would be responsible for the snowstorm over the central
Great Plains, Upper Mississippi valley, and Upper Michigan
from May 27 through May 29. A strong Arctic high-pressure
system was located over the Mackenzie Basin in northwest
Canada. This high-pressure system would provide the cold
air needed for a winter storm to build. A mixture of rain and
snow developed over Colorado and Wyoming during the
day on May 27 and changed to all snow during the night as
the low deepened and moved slowly east through southern
Colorado.

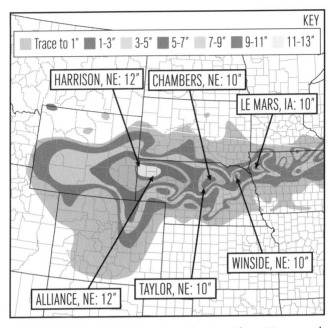

33. May 27–29, 1947, snowfall totals in the Great Plains. Map created by Katie Nieland with information from the National Weather Service, http://www.weather.gov/arx/may27291947snow.

On the morning of the May 28, the high-pressure center had moved rapidly south to southern Saskatchewan. This high-pressure area brought unprecedented cold for late May to North Dakota. Temperatures fell to as low as 15° at Eckman, which is located near the Canadian border. In addition, the mercury fell to 23° at Bismarck, which is the lowest ever recorded for so late in the season. Meanwhile, below-freezing temperatures were found across Montana, Wyoming, northeastern Colorado, western Nebraska, northern Minnesota, and western South Dakota. The subfreezing temperatures caused a partial to total loss of fruits and tender plants. During the day, this cold air surged southward across eastern Nebraska, eastern South Dakota, Iowa, southern Minnesota, and Wisconsin. Many record-cold daily high temperatures were established across the region for the day. That is, daily high temperatures this cold had not been recorded so late into the spring previous to this storm.

At the same time, the area of low pressure was continuing to strengthen as it moved east through southern Kansas. From the evening of May 27 through May 28 this low produced a six-to-twelve-inch snow band from southeast Wyoming east across northern Nebraska into northwest Iowa (see figure 33 for a map charting these snowfall totals across the region). The heaviest snow in this band was found in Alliance and Harrison, Nebraska, where twelve inches had fallen. The weight from the heavy wet snow caused considerable damage to power lines, telephone lines, telegraph lines, trees, and shrubs.

Ice Storms

The Great Plains is in a perfect location for the occurrence of ice storms. The gently rolling landscape provides no barrier to the northward-moving, warm moist Gulf air riding up over the top of the shallow polar and Arctic air moving toward the south (see figure 34 describing precipitation types and how they are created). Blizzards and snowstorms can paralyze a region and halt all transportation, but at least, given some time, the snow can be removed from the highways and airports so that transportation can resume its normal course. Ice storms, however, cannot be plowed or moved to the side of a road. Power lines can become loaded with the heavy weight of ice and come crashing down to the ground, ripping tree branches along the away and plunging areas into total darkness as electrical lines are snapped. The only way to remove the accumulation of ice blanketing a portion of the Great Plains is to have the sun

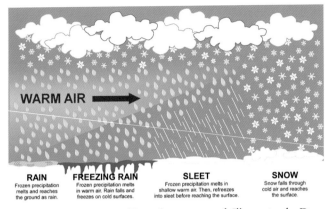

34. Precipitation types and how they are created. Illustration by Dee Ebbeka.

appear along with above-freezing temperatures. During these ice storm events, the residents of the Great Plains experiencing heavy snowfall should feel grateful that they are just north of the zone of ice accumulation.

Ice Storm in Lincoln, Nebraska, January 2017

Saturday January 14, 2017, was a pleasant midwinter day in Lincoln, Nebraska, with a high temperature of 39° and with abundant sunshine. The landscape was brown with no snow cover, and it appeared like winter was going to skip our area here in Lincoln. Sunday, January 15, started out partly sunny, but moisture-rich clouds began to spread north from the Gulf of Mexico into southern Nebraska by late morning. The temperature by midafternoon had only risen to 31°, and then it began, around 3:00 p.m. The ground, sidewalks, and streets were all just below freezing in temperature when a steady rain began to fall. Warm air had wedged over the region so that snow falling from upper levels in the clouds was melting into rain and falling through a shallow layer of cold air just above the surface. Since the surface temperature was below freezing, the rain froze on contact, creating a frozen landscape.

Recognizing that this was a long-term event expected to last twenty-four hours or more, local radio station KLIN contacted me and I began to give live hourly updates on the developing ice storm to the listeners from my house. I took occasional photos outside my house and pushed them out to the social media. The temperature did not change from 31° all afternoon, throughout the evening, and all night long. I stopped giving hourly media updates for a few hours and resumed again the next morning, Monday, January 16. At dawn it was still 31°. The temperature in Lincoln rose only one degree to 32° by 9:00 a.m. and stayed at that temperature for the rest of the calendar day and into the early-morning hours of the next day.

The ice accumulation could have been much worse. We had a total of 0.81 inches of liquid water, but due to the temperature hovering so close to freezing, much of the water did not freeze to surfaces but ran off. Can you imagine what would have happened had the entire amount of water, almost an inch, stuck to all of the surfaces (especially trees and power lines). The morning of Tuesday, January 17, started out briefly shrouded in fog and clouds, but by 9:00 a.m. the clouds and fog began to dissipate and the sun came out glinting on an ice-covered landscape. As I have done throughout my career, with a smile on my face, I grabbed a camera and went outside to take photos of our "winter wonderland" landscape (see figure 35).

Of all the forms of winter weather that impact the Great Plains, ice storms strike the most fear for its residents. Although the January 2017 ice storm in Lincoln had a minimal impact and had its photographic beauty, this is not always the case. When major ice storms impact an area, chipping ice off of car windows can take hours of labor. Hospital emergency rooms can fill with people coming in with broken bones from slipping and falling

35. January 17, 2017, following the ice storm in Lincoln, Nebraska. Photo by the author.

on ice-covered surfaces. Freezing rain and ice accumulation can cause rural power lines to crash to the surface, knocking out electricity and leaving homes in the dark for days. Without electricity, furnaces can't turn on to provide heat. In urban areas, ice accumulation can bring large tree branches down, causing significant damage to both cars and houses. The impact of an ice storm can last for prolonged periods.

Some of the nation's worst ice storms have occurred on the plains. The National Weather Service at the Wichita, Kansas, office produced a summary listing the top five worst ice storms in the state of Kansas (https://www.weather.gov/ict/ks_worse _ice_storms):

December 10–11, 2007:

Nearly all of Kansas

Ice accumulation 2 to 4 inches

Power outages 1–2 weeks, some areas longer

Electrical infrastructure damage: $136.2 million

January 29–31, 2002:

Southwest, south-central, and all of eastern Kansas

Ice accumulation 1 to 4 inches

Power outages 1 to 2 weeks

Total of all damage: estimated at $60 million

January 4–5, 2005:

Nearly all of Kansas

Ice accumulation ½ to 2 inches

Power outages 1½ to 2 weeks

Total of all damage: estimated at $36 million

March 18–19, 1984:

Southwest to northeast Kansas

Ice accumulation 1 to 2 inches

Power outages 1 week, some locations a little longer

82 percent of Topeka was without power

Damage in Topeka: estimated to be worse than the June 8, 1996, (E)F5 tornado

March 15–17, 1998:

Southwest to north-central Kansas

Ice accumulation ½ to 6 inches

Power outages up to a week

Total of all damage: estimated at $3.5 million

On December 29–31, 2006, a significant ice storm paralyzed south-central Nebraska with several inches of ice accumulating

36. December 2006 ice storm in central Nebraska. Photo courtesy of NOAA, December 29–31, 2006, ice storm photo gallery.

on exposed surfaces (figure 36 shows a photo of an ice-covered tree near Kearney).

A total of 1.48 inches of liquid precipitation fell during this event with near-surface and surface temperatures well below freezing. According to the Hastings, Nebraska, National Weather Service office (https://www.weather.gov/gid/2006 _icestorm), "These ice accumulations caused widespread damage to trees, power lines, and power poles. Even large metal power structures were crumpled to the ground. Several small towns and rural residences relied on generators for electric power, in some cases for weeks." A few months later, NOAA's *Storm Data* journal included the following from the NWS Omaha/ Valley storm episode narrative:

> In total over Nebraska, the ice storm knocked 37 main high-voltage transmission lines across 600 miles out of

service, snapped or toppled more than 6,000 utility poles, including large steel structures, caused power outages for over 15,000 homes and businesses in over 30 communities and did an estimated $240 million in utility damage alone. Some towns remained without power for days afterward, and some more remote customers remained without power for weeks. A major disaster declaration was issued for 57 counties in Nebraska from this storm. As of late January 2007, the state was to receive $30 million, slightly more than the total received by the state for the previous 16 federal disaster declarations dating back to 1990.

CHAPTER FIVE

The Endless Cycle from Droughts to Floods

The geography of the Great Plains creates an environment that naturally has extremes in precipitation. Arid and semi-arid conditions exist just to the west of the Great Plains, and humid moisture-rich environments can be found just to the east of the Great Plains. As noted earlier, air masses can easily approach and sweep over the barrier-free Great Plains from all directions. If the air masses don't "take turns," and either arid or humid air masses begin to dominate the weather pattern, the Great Plains can easily move into an arid drought cycle or a moisture-rich, humid flood-producing cycle. It is not surprising, then, that the annual precipitation on the Great Plains has an extreme variability, unlike anywhere else in the United States. For example, Bismarck, North Dakota, has seen annual precipitation as low as 5.97 inches (1936) to as much as 30.92 inches (1876), a difference of 517.9 percent (see figure 37 for a table of precipitation extremes on the Great Plains).

A transect of the Great Plains from North Dakota to Texas illustrates the extreme variability in precipitation, with the wettest years being as much as 566 percent wetter than the driest years. No wonder, then, that the Great Plains precipitation

LOCATION	DRIEST	YEAR	WETTEST	YEAR	% DIFFERENCE
BISMARK, ND	5.97	1936	30.92	1876	517.9
ABERDEEN, SD	7.72	1976	42.12	1896	545.6
GRAND ISLAND, NE	11.58	2012	45.50	1905	392.9
DODGE CITY, KS	9.98	1956	33.61	1944	336.8
OKLAHOMA CITY, OK	15.74	1901	56.97	2007	361.9
AMARILLO, TX	7.02	2011	39.75	1923	566.2
ABILENE, TX	9.79	1956	48.77	1941	498.2

37. Precipitation extremes in the Great Plains (in inches). Table created by Alexa Horn with information from the High Plains Regional Climate Center.

can endlessly cycle back and forth from extreme droughts to flooding. But is this extreme variability predictable?

Although many people have tried to find a drought cycle to better forecast this variation, there is in fact no predictable regularity to these events. When I first moved to the Great Plains, the public would often tell me that there was a regular twenty-two-year drought cycle on the plains. However, I have never found evidence of a regular drought cycle in any of the climate data archives. Figure 38 graphs these data, extending back over 118 years to 1900, dramatically illustrating that there is no predictable regularity of drought cycles on the plains. Some of the droughts are intense but only short lived, while others have lasted for several years and some as long as a decade or even longer.

Typically, drought "creeps up" on the residents of the Great Plains. That is, the droughts develop slowly over a period of several months. However, the Great Plains region is also subject to rapid-onset droughts that are termed "flash droughts." The recent 2012 flash drought on the Great Plains is an example of these intense, rapidly developing droughts.

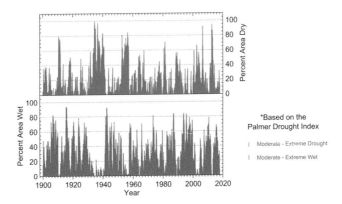

38. Percentage of extreme drought and extreme wet areas in the Great Plains, January 1900 to December 2017. Courtesy of NOAA.

The graph in figure 39 shows the monthly percentage of the high plains region that was in drought across several years. Looking at just the 2011 to 2015 time period, it becomes obvious that a flash drought occurred on the Great Plains in 2012. On May 1, 2012, there was very little drought across the plains from northeast Texas all the way north to the Dakotas. However, drought conditions rapidly developed, and by July 3, only eight weeks later, almost the entire Great Plains was experiencing drought. By September 4, not only was the entire Great Plains region in drought conditions, a large portion of the region had the drought magnitude intensify to "Exceptional Drought." Agricultural producers went into their growing season in 2012 with conditions looking quite favorable; however, massive crop failures occurred with this rapidly developing flash drought.

Of further interest, while the graph might seem to suggest that a flash drought was developing at the start of the high plains growing season in 2015, as drought conditions rapidly developed, closer inspection of the data shows that by the middle of

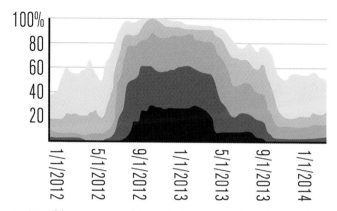

39. Monthly percentage of the high plains region that is in drought for the period January 2012 to January 2014. Graph courtesy of the National Drought Mitigation Center, http://droughtmonitor.unl.edu/Data/Timeseries.aspx.

the growing season, drought conditions had virtually vanished in the region. These rapid and extreme changes in drought conditions create a nightmare for water management agencies trying to anticipate water releases ahead of time for irrigation across the region.

The National Drought Mitigation Center

Given the possibility of drought across the plains states, it is not a surprise to find that the National Drought Mitigation Center (NDMC) is located at the University of Nebraska–Lincoln. The NDMC was established in 1995 to help reduce the nation's vulnerability to drought. It works with states and tribal governments across the United States and with national governments around the world to develop better drought risk management strategies. These include monitoring, early warning, and planning, as opposed to crisis management.

The NDMC is divided into two main drought research program areas: (1) Monitoring, and (2) Planning and Social Science. NDMC climatologists are actively researching the best ways to monitor and communicate about drought. They work with other researchers across the country and around the world on drought monitoring and agricultural meteorology. The NDMC's Planning and Social Science team primarily focuses on drought planning, research, education, and facilitating stakeholder involvement. The team has experience helping planners learn exactly how drought has affected an area in the past, how it's likely to affect them in the future, and what steps can be taken to implement best-management practices and develop drought plans.

The NDMC also maintains an extensive website with resources for monitoring, assessing impacts, planning, and K-12 education. More information about NDMC can be found at http://drought.unl.edu/.

The Dust Bowl, aka the "Dirty Thirties"

The decade of the 1930s was a period of prolonged drought in the Great Plains with very few areas of excessive wet conditions. The Native Americans who lived on the Great Plains lived in relative harmony with the extremes in weather and climate. However, the Homestead Act of 1862, which provided settlers with 160 acres of public land on the Great Plains, and the expanded Homestead Act of 1909 set in motion an environmental nightmare that finally reared its ugly head in the 1930s. Multigenerational families migrated from eastern and western Europe in response to this opportunity for free agricultural land and the opportunity to farm. Even today it is still possible to find communities on the Great Plains that have a predominant German, Swedish, Danish, Czech, and Basque immigrant history with annual festivals celebrating their

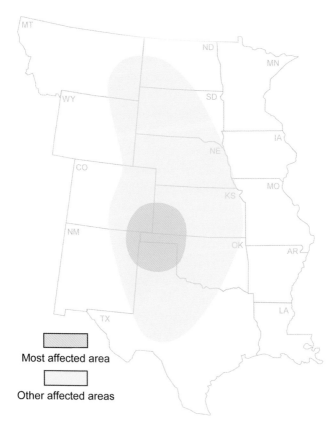

Most affected area

Other affected areas

40. The geographic extent of the Dust Bowl during the decade of
1930s. Map created by the author.

European heritage. Unfortunately, these farmers brought with
them European farming techniques. The climate back home
was nowhere near as variable and extreme as what they would
experience here on the plains.

Another migration was taking place at this same time in the
form of wagon trains taking large groups of emigrants westward
across the Great Plains headed toward California. During the

drought periods, emigrants passing through this region referred to the western part of the Great Plains, east of the Rocky Mountains and west of approximately the hundredth meridian, as the "Great American Desert." Today this same region is often referred to as the "high plains."

Many of the new homesteaders bought into the myth that "rain follows the plow" and actually believed that turning the soil over and growing plants would increase rainfall. Despite their hope for an agricultural paradise, the families homesteading on the Great Plains found extreme precipitation variability from year to year and the occurrence of multiyear droughts.

One of these multiyear droughts occurred from 1930 to 1939 and is commonly referred to as the Dust Bowl (see figure 40 for the geographic extent of the Dust Bowl during the 1930s).

The Nebraska state high of 118° was set on July 24, 1936 in Minden, Nebraska (roughly fifty miles southwest of Grand Island). And, in fact, many of the Great Plains states experienced their all-time, record-high temperatures during the 1930s. Listed from north to south, here are the state record-high temperatures and the towns recording them:

Steele, North Dakota: 121°, July 6, 1936

Gannvalley, South Dakota: 120°, July 5, 1936 (tied again on July 15, 2006)

Minden, Nebraska: 118°, July 24, 1936

Alton, Kansas: 121°, July 24, 1936

Altus, Oklahoma: 120°, July 18, 19, August 10, 12, 1936, and at three other locations (tied again on June 27, 1994)

Seymour, Texas: 120°, August 12, 1936 (tied again on June 28, 1994)

Nebraska had a statewide average of 22 inches of moisture in 1930 with an average of 25 bushels per acre for their corn

41. A dust storm moves across the plains during the 1930s. Courtesy of the Kansas State Historical Society.

crop. However, during 1934, Nebraska had its driest year on record with a statewide average of only 14.5 inches of moisture and the state's corn crop dropped over 75 percent to only 6.2 bushels per acre.

Many historic photographs from this time show a harsh nightmarish scene of "black (topsoil-laden) blizzards" (similar to the dust cloud of a haboob) rolling across the state (see figure 41). Timothy Egan's book *The Worst Hard Time* provides an excellent description of this harsh period as told in the words of those who survived the Great American Dust Bowl. One of these particularly awful dust storms is referred to as Black Sunday, which took place on April 14, 1935. A total of twenty dust storms occurred in the Dust Bowl region on this day. In many locations, day turned into night with dark swirling clouds of dust

The book and movie *The Grapes of Wrath* chronicles the outmigration of families that took place during the Dust Bowl. This decade of the Dust Bowl saw a sharp decrease in population, especially in the hardest-hit drought areas of the Great Plains.

Over three hundred thousand people left the Great Plains, mostly for the West Coast and California.

It was during this decade-long Dust Bowl that the U.S. government saw the importance of preventing environmental disasters and began to institute several government policies. The Emergency Farm Mortgage Act was passed in 1933. The Soil Conservation Program was established in 1935. The Great Plains Shelterbelt program was initiated in 1934 by President Franklin D. Roosevelt. This project encouraged farmers to create windbreaks, that is, rows of trees on the perimeters of farms, hoping to reduce wind velocity and lessen evaporation of moisture from the soil. The project stretched from North Dakota to northern Texas and helped stabilize soil and rejuvenate farm communities affected by the dust storms.

Flooding on the Great Plains

The Great Plains is clearly the heartland of extremes in the U.S. As the chapter title implies, the climate here swings back and forth between too little precipitation and too much. And unfortunately, without any regular cycle, it is difficult for plains residents to anticipate either of these extremes. Droughts can develop over a period of months and last for years; however, the time frame for flooding is much different.

There are several ways flooding can happen on the Great Plains. Excessive snow cover with rapid warming and melting in late winter and early spring can quickly push rivers out of their banks and flood low-lying areas. Another late winter–early spring flooding event is caused by ice chunks breaking up on rivers and, while flowing downstream, getting caught at bridges and bends in the river blocking the free flow of the river. Water begins to back up quickly upstream, and in the period of just a few hours water can surge out of riverbanks and into surrounding areas.

Weather patterns can also get "stuck" with repeated rainfall over an area over a period of weeks to several months. Late spring into summer 1993 was an example of much of the plains becoming waterlogged with rivers in flood stage for several months. A feedback loop was also at work during this situation since the daily, hot summer temperatures over the waterlogged soils ensured copious amounts of evaporation, which resulted in increased frequency of clouds and thunderstorms, keeping the cycle alive and persisting for weeks. The most dramatic type of flooding on the Great Plains is the flash flood, where intense convective thunderstorms can turn small creeks and rivers into raging torrents and convert urban roads into temporary rivers. These flash floods typically last for just a few hours to at most about a day as the localized rainfall works its way into the surrounding stream network. It should be pointed out that urban areas respond differently than rural areas to these types of floods, with the hard impervious surfaces of the urban area reaching flash-flood conditions more quickly and shedding the flood water more quickly. Many larger urban areas have "urban search and rescue" teams that are trained to rescue urban motorists and residents that get caught in flash floods (see figure 42).

Although these types of flooding have occurred on a regular basis throughout the plains, there are notable floods that have occurred throughout its history.

The Missouri River Flood of 1881

The winter of 1880–81 was unusually cold and saw very deep snow cover across the upper Great Plains and Missouri River basin. Ice thickness was in excess of two feet in the Missouri River between Yankton, South Dakota, and Omaha, Nebraska. Ironically, the spring thaw began first in the upper portion of the Missouri basin, resulting in water flowing southward to where the river was still deeply frozen. The ice finally began to break up

42. Urban search-and-rescue team looking for people stranded by flooding in Kingfisher, Oklahoma. Courtesy of FEMA/Marvin Nauman.

in the lower portion of the Missouri basin and the deep snow cover began to melt rapidly, resulting in the largest Missouri River discharge (until 1952). According to David Pearson, of the NWS Omaha office, several Nebraska towns were washed away. The flooding at the town of Niobrara was so extreme that the town was moved to a new location on higher ground. Flooding in Omaha reached up to Ninth Street, and Council Bluffs, Iowa, was inundated with flood water as the Missouri River spread out across its flood plain. Although this historical flood is buried in the record books, and few area residents are likely aware that it ever occurred, it was a significant flood for an important reason. This magnitude of a flood was used as a guide when designing the six Missouri River main-stem dams.

Republican River Flood of 1935

The concept of the Great Plains being a location of weather and climate extremes was dramatically illustrated during the

Republican River flood in Nebraska in 1935, which ironically occurred during the peak of the Dust Bowl, the driest decade on record for Nebraska and the Great Plains.

From May 30 to June 2, 1935, persistent thunderstorms dropped nine to twenty-four inches of rain across eastern Colorado and other areas of the upper Republican River basin. The resulting flood devastated a wide swath downriver. Cambridge, Nebraska, the most affected, had 75 percent of its homes flooded. A total of ninety-four people were killed, and 307 bridges were damaged beyond repair or completely destroyed and could no longer be used. There are many stories of people clinging to trees until they could be rescued. The area suffered more than $26 million in Depression-era dollar losses ($440 million in 2013 dollars).

The public demand for flood control and more efficient irrigation helped urge Congress to pass the 1944 Flood Control Act that authorized construction of dams in the Republican River basin.

In addition to the flooding during this event, violent thunderstorms on May 31, 1935, produced a tornado near McCook, Nebraska, killing five people and injuring thirty-five (see figure 43). Two more people were killed just east of Lexington, Nebraska, as these intense thunderstorms roared through this part of Nebraska. Most people are familiar with the phrase "adding insult to injury," and this is exactly what happened on that day as a dust storm from Oklahoma passed through McCook at the peak of the flood.

Missouri River Flooding of 1952

The snowfall and snow depth during the winter of 1951–52 was well above normal. This, combined with well above normal temperatures, in April 1952, resulted in a rapid melting of the snowpack. Fortunately, there was enough advance warning so

43. Historical photo showing the May 31, 1935, flooding in Nebraska with a person using a rope line to be rescued from the flooded building. Courtesy of the Nebraska State Historical Society.

that Omaha-area levees could be raised higher. Troops were brought into the area and sandbags were added to the existing levees raising their height to 33.5 feet, which turned out to be about 4 feet above the peak flood discharge. The Missouri River spread out across the floodplain increasing its width in some places to sixteen miles wide. Although the levees held, protecting almost all of downtown Omaha, there was still almost $2 million in damage to Omaha streets south of downtown and along the Missouri River. Carter Lake, just north of Omaha, did not fare as well as Omaha and had to be evacuated as the community became inundated with flood water. Reporter Bill Billotte, of the *Omaha World Herald* (http://www.omahahistory.org), reported that he was told by a levee worker, "We threw a dozen bags of sand in there, and the river threw them right back at us."

Stockville, Nebraska, Flood of June 21, 1947

Although, it wasn't really notable as a significant Great Plains flood event, I included this flood in the book since it impacted my son-in-law John Heaston's family. John and Mary Harbert (grandparents of John Heaston and parents of his mother, Barbara) lived along Medicine Creek, just north of Stockville, Nebraska. On the night of June 21, 1947, thunderstorms converged on the area north of Curtis, Nebraska. The closest location with archived climate data is Curtis, and the climate records show that the town received 5.10 inches of rain that evening. It is not inconceivable that there were amounts well in excess of that amount but went unrecorded with a lack of official data-collection locations in that area. The wall of flood water worked its way south toward Stockville, destroying bridges along the way.

John Harbert's sister Luella was visiting from nearby North Platte, with her infant daughter, whose fussing was keeping her awake in the middle of that night. While tending to her, she heard water dripping somewhere in the house. She was unable to find the source of the dripping water until a flash of lightning outside briefly illuminated the room and she saw that water was dripping into the room through the keyhole in the front door. The water was quickly rising and she alerted the family of the imminent danger. They gathered on the second floor of the house as it began to shift from the foundation and float up against a creek bank. The family escaped the house through the second-floor window and onto the nearby creek bank. Shortly after that, their house shifted further down the creek and lodged in a group of trees downstream.

My son-in-law's grandparents were lucky, but there were others who were not as fortunate. There were nine fatalities from this flash flood with four people missing and never found. A total of 150 homes were flooded, many of them totally destroyed, and 196 people were rescued from their flooded homes. Much of this information comes from the publication *Stockville, Then and Now*, compiled in 1999 by members of the Stockville Women's Club.

Frequent Springtime Flooding of the Red River of the North

Almost all rivers in the United States flow toward warmer locations, but an interesting geographic fact about the Red River in the northern Great Plains of North Dakota is that it flows northward. This by itself doesn't seem all that significant, but during the spring melt season the river heads north into a colder climate before the spring thaw has occurred there. If the snow cover in North Dakota melts too quickly, massive volumes of water attempt to enter the frozen landscape of southern Manitoba. The forward movement of the Red River can find itself blocked and water begins to back up, flooding the northeastern North Dakota towns located along its banks. In addition to this problem, as the ice on the river begins to break up south of this area, ice jams begin to occur where water is still flowing, causing localized overflows of water from the river. There are several low-level bridges that have been constructed in this area and they are especially prone to ice jams.

The Red River valley is in one of the flattest terrains in the U.S., located in an ancient lake bed known as Glacial Lake Agassiz. When the river goes into flood stage onto this plain, it can spread out dramatically over a large area since it is a nearly flat plain. The river dynamics here are the opposite of mountainous rapids with steep gradients; with a drop in elevation of only 5 inches per mile in the Fargo area and as little as 1.5 inches per mile as it approaches the Canadian border, a river with such a small gradient is naturally going to be slow moving, allowing flooding to persist for prolonged periods of time. As the flood water spreads out onto the basically flat surface, the region becomes, in essence, a massive, shallow lake.

During recent years in Fargo, the Red River has passed into flood stage at least once per year. During most years, this flooding has been minor. However, since 1993, several of these floods

44. A flooded city center of Grand Forks, North Dakota, in April 1997. Courtesy of NOAA, https://www.weather.gov/safety/flood -states-nd.

have been truly devastating, especially the epic 1997 flood. The largest city impacted by a flooding Red River is Grand Forks, North Dakota.

The 1997 event flooded roughly 85 percent of the city of Grand Forks, along with smaller North Dakota and Minnesota communities (see figure 44). Rural areas along the Red River and its tributaries suffered significant damage as well.

On April 18, 1997, the peak stage of the Red River of the North at Grand Forks was 52.04 feet, which is 1.84 feet higher than the record set in 1897, and the peak flow was 137,000 cubic feet per second. The peak flow was unusual because it resulted from the convergence of flows from the Red Lake River in Minnesota, flows from the main channel, and breakout flows from the Red River of the North that were conveyed by old Red River of the North abandoned channels known as "oxbows." Breakout flows occurred upstream from Grand Forks when plugs in the upstream end of these oxbows either were overtopped or washed away, which caused a flow of about 25,000 cubic feet per second to arrive at the confluence of the Red Lake River and the Red River of the North at Grand Forks. The flow of 25,000 cubic feet per second coincided with the peak flow of the two rivers.

To compound problems in Grand Forks, a fire the next day, on April 19, demolished several buildings in the flooded city. The flooding made it extremely difficult for firefighters to reach the fires and put them out. Except for emergency personnel, Grand Forks and its sister city, East Grand Forks, Minnesota, were completely evacuated at this time. The damage inflicted to one of North Dakota's largest communities prompted a federal flood protection project for the cities of Grand Forks and East Grand Forks.

The Two-Part 1993 Flooding in Southeastern Nebraska

In the spring of 1993, over two feet of snow fell across southeastern Nebraska between January and early March. Spring warmth had been late in returning to the region, arriving well into March, when suddenly temperatures warmed into the mid- to upper 70s in late March. With great sighs of relief, the residents of the eastern Great Plains greeted the annual return of southerly winds bringing up warmer air from the south. However, it also brought early spring rains into the area, dropping several inches of rain onto the landscape. The Platte River had to take on this extra runoff and, combined with the late thaw of the river, the Platte quickly moved into flood stage. The ice on the river began to break up, but not before ice jams began to form at bends in the river and at bridges. It wasn't long before residents living along the Platte River between Columbus and Ashland were forced from their homes. Water began to flow across farm fields and across county and state roads.

Eventually, the Platte River flood water blocked by the ice jams began to flood Interstate 80 north of where it normally crosses under the highway. The major transportation corridor shut down for almost a week as the water remained high over the interstate. The Army Corps of Engineers tried dropping explosive charges into the ice jams but it was to no avail. I spent several days in warm springtime temperatures photographing this flooding, and eventually the warm temperatures began to melt the ice jams and they broke up and headed downstream toward the Missouri River. Debris was plowed off of I-80 just north of the Platte River for several miles, and it looked strange piled up along the side of the road like rows of snow but consisting instead of river-transported debris, including many small tree branches.

Heading into late spring and early summer of 1993, the eastern and southern Missouri River basin in Iowa, Nebraska, South Dakota, Kansas, and Missouri had transformed to nearly water-saturated soil conditions. This is also climatologically the wettest time of the year, with average May precipitation as much as five times greater than average January precipitation. This meant that there was little storage room in the soil for these rains, and river levels remained high heading into June. A meteorological "feedback mechanism" began to take place across this saturated region. Daily heating would evaporate water into the overlying atmosphere creating clouds feeding afternoon thunderstorms that repeatedly dropped heavy rain across the waterlogged landscape. Looking at data from the High Plains Regional Climate Center, precipitation totals exceeded 200 percent of normal across much of this area. Falls City, Nebraska, with a normal July precipitation of just under 5 inches, received 25.29 inches of rain in July 1993 (more than 500 percent of normal).

But it wasn't just the amount of rainfall that was of note; it was also the persistence of rain events, never letting the area dry out. Rain fell somewhere in the Missouri River basin every day from mid-March to late July in 1993. The Missouri River reached record crests during the third week in July with several levees overtopped between Brownville, Nebraska, and St. Joseph, Missouri. According to David Pearson, N W S hydrologist at the Omaha/Valley office, damage totaled $44 million ($71 million in 2013 dollars), and 5.8 million acres of cropland were flooded resulting in $317 million dollars in damage ($512 million in 2013 dollars).

And then, as so often happens on the Great Plains, the rain virtually stopped falling from late July into the autumn. River levels began to fall, slowly at first and then more rapidly, and the fields that were under water for months dried out and actually had cracks in the soil by September. The fine sediment transported by the flood waters and deposited across the region now became airborne, with fine dust being picked up from the fields by the wind and blown into the air by vehicles driving the once-flooded rural roads. As I traveled into the area several months later, clouds of dust would swirl behind my car and I couldn't get close to any vehicle in front of me since visibility was greatly reduced by the vehicle stirring up the fine sediment dust. You can read more about this flooding event on the website of the National Oceanic and Atmospheric Administration: http://www.nws.noaa.gov/om/assessments/pdfs/93_Flood.pdf

Urban Flooding in Lincoln, Nebraska, May 2015

May 6–7, 2015, saw almost ten inches of rain falling in four hours in southeast Nebraska over a localized area centered on the Salt Creek watershed. All of the water in this watershed headed northeast, with Lincoln in the way. There was localized flooding the evening before in Lincoln during the height of the storm, but that water had drained off the roads well before dawn. Shortly after sunrise the flood wave of water from the

45. Antelope Creek flood diversion in effect in Lincoln, Nebraska, on May 7, 2015. Photo by the author.

south reached Lincoln and the Salt Creek overflowed its banks in Wilderness Park in southwest Lincoln, blocking some of the roads in that area. Students who had parked at nearby Southwest High School in Lincoln looked out the windows and under bright blue sunny skies saw water rising into the school parking lots. They scrambled outside along with teachers to move their vehicles to higher ground. Areas in the near south neighborhood of Lincoln began to flood and rescue workers began to remove residents from that area to higher ground. The surge of flood water overtopped the levees just west of the University of Nebraska–Lincoln campus and began to spread across the parking lots and into the baseball stadium located on the western edge of the campus.

Antelope Creek (a tributary to Salt Creek) passes through the center of Lincoln and is part of Lincoln's urban flood-control system. Flood water from southeast Lincoln was still discharging into Antelope Creek that morning, and as that water reached

46. Antelope Creek, on May 10, 2015, a few days after the urban flash flooding in Lincoln, Nebraska, and at the same location as the photo in figure 45. Photo by the author.

its merger with Salt Creek, just north of the university campus, there was nowhere for the Antelope Creek water to go. The Antelope Creek flood-control system was barely able to handle this increased volume of water. What a startling contrast from the normal trickle of water that passes through Antelope Creek. When I went over to the creek to take photos, I found students canoeing on the now-flooded creek (see figures 45 and 46).

CHAPTER SIX

Tornadoes on the Great Plains

My first association of tornadoes with the Great Plains came when I saw the movie *The Wizard of Oz* for the first time as a child and watched in awe as Dorothy Gale (Judy Garland) was swept away from a farm in Kansas to a magical Land of Oz in a tornado. But it is more than a movie that creates this association in the minds of the public. The wide open spaces of the plains has allowed for many tornadoes to be easily photographed and seen in news broadcasts and in print form in newspapers, magazines, and books. During my travels across the plains, I have heard many residents brag about the F-Scale of a tornado that came through their area. What is this scale that causes people to proudly say, for example "We survived an F-4 tornado"?

The Fujita Tornado Scale

Dr. T. Theodore Fujita, meteorologist at the University of Chicago, first introduced the Fujita Scale (F-Scale) in 1971. Dr. Fujita's goals in his research in developing the F-Scale were to categorize each tornado by its intensity, size (area), and estimated wind speed associated with the damage caused by the tornado. The F-Scale then became the heart of the tornado database that contains a record of every known tornado in the United States since 1950. The F-Scale was

U.S. Tornadoes

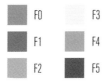

■	F0	□	F3
■	F1	■	F4
■	F2	■	F5

Total tornadoes by category (1950 - 2016)

Total occurances: 58,274

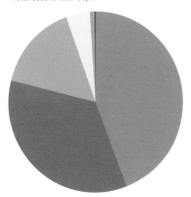

U.S. Tornado Fatalities (1950 - 2016)

Total fatalities: 6,081

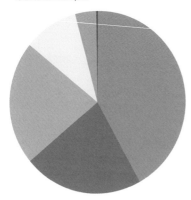

47. Tornado data have been collected only since the early 1950s. There are 58,274 tornadoes in the 1950–2016 data archive. Charts created by Katie Nieland with information from the Storm Prediction Center, National Severe Weather Database Browser, Online Severe Plot 3.0.

replaced with the Enhanced Fujita Scale or EF-Scale, which became operational on February 1, 2007. When the new scale was adopted, it was agreed that there must be conformity with the F-Scale that is listed in the database. The data set utilized in this book is a combination of the two scales with the assumption that for example, F-4 tornadoes in the past can be combined with the more recent EF-4 tornadoes for mapping and analysis.

There is a dramatic difference between the frequency of tornado intensities (as each tornado is ranked on the six-point Enhanced Fujita Scale) and the frequency of tornado-caused fatalities. Figure 47 shows that there were a total of 58,274 tornadoes in the 1950–2016 data archive. While 46,066 (79 percent) of all of these tornadoes were ranked EF-0 plus EF-1, they accounted for only 255 (4.2 percent) of all of the tornado-related fatalities. In contrast, there were only 639 (1.1 percent) of all the tornadoes occurring during this time period that were ranked EF-4 plus EF-5, and yet they accounted for 3,876 (63.8 percent) of all of the tornado-related fatalities.

Tornado Trends

There has been a significant overall trend of increasing numbers of tornadoes for the United States (all F-Scale values combined). However, there has been no increasing trend among the stronger EF-3 to EF-5 tornadoes. There has also been no increase in the number of days with tornadoes on an annual basis (see figure 48 for a graph mapping these data). Scientists have concluded that almost all of the apparent increase is due to enhanced public awareness and better reporting methods during the last few decades as well as the increased number of people who are engaged in "storm chasing" and observing smaller tornadoes that in the past went unreported.

Frequency of U.S. Tornadoes, 1950-2016

All tornadoes versus severe tornadoes, (E)F scale

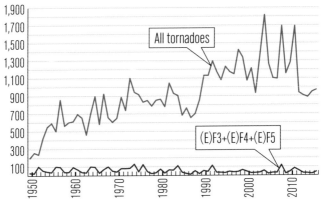

48. Annual total of all tornadoes compared to the total of all severe tornadoes rated as E F - 3 and higher. Blue line is all tornadoes and red line is E F - 3 and higher tornadoes. Graph created by Katie Nieland with information from the Storm Prediction Center, N O A A, Severe Plot program, http://www.spc.noaa.gov/climo/online/sp3/plot.php.

The Seasonality of Great Plains Tornadoes

Similar to the climatology of hail frequency on the Great Plains, the seasonal peak in tornado occurrence happens much earlier on the southern Great Plains compared to the northern Great Plains. The peak in tornado frequency also occurs during the month of May, just as for hail occurrences. The region of highest frequencies of tornado occurrence is located over central Oklahoma and into northern Texas in April and May, but has moved northward into northeast Colorado and much of Nebraska by June. July and August see a greatly reduced probability of tornadoes on the Great Plains and they are primarily limited to the central and northern Great Plains.

Where, Exactly, Is Tornado Alley?

The term "Tornado Alley" was first used in 1952 by U.S. Air Force meteorologists Major Ernest J. Fawbush and Captain C. Robert Miller as the title of a research project to study severe weather in parts of Texas and Oklahoma.

However, defining the exact geographic area of Tornado Alley is similar to trying to define the exact geographic limits of the Great Plains. Many Tornado Alley maps have been created over the years. Most maps outline the region from northeast Texas up through Nebraska and slightly east into Iowa as Tornado Alley. There are maps showing the geographic extent of Tornado Alley extending further north up into the Dakotas, and some maps extend Tornado Alley out of the Great Plains to the east into Illinois and Indiana. This definition does ignore the high frequency of tornadoes across the Gulf States into Florida. I have seen the phrase "Dixie Alley" used to describe this second area of high tornado frequency, but it has never stuck with the public or the media, and instead when they hear Tornado Alley, they automatically think of the Great Plains region from Texas to Nebraska.

These two Tornado Alleys become obvious when looking at the tornado data. The Storm Prediction Center maintains an archive of all verified tornado occurrences since 1950. Looking at the most recent thirty-year period (1987–2016) the annual average tornado frequency for each state was standardized using a scale of number of tornadoes per 10,000 square miles. The top thirteen standardized tornado frequencies include the following:

Traditional Tornado Alley, into the Midwest:

Kansas: 11 tornadoes per 10,000 square miles

Illinois: 10 tornadoes per 10,000 square miles

Oklahoma and Iowa: 9 tornadoes per 10,000 square miles

Nebraska and Indiana: 7 tornadoes per 10,000 square miles

Dixie Alley:

Mississippi, Florida and Alabama: 10 tornadoes per 10,000 square miles

Louisiana, South Carolina, Tennessee, Arkansas: 8 tornadoes per 10,000 square miles

These numbers illustrate that the tornado frequency peak is spread out not only across the classic Tornado Alley but also into the region off to the east and southeast as well.

The map in figure 49—with 13,454 tornadoes mapped for a recent ten-year period—illustrates that tornadoes in the conterminous U.S. are active not only within the traditional Tornado Alley region in the Great Plains but also throughout the Midwest and across the Gulf States. It appears that the attribution of the phrase Tornado Alley for the Great Plains region is more of a convenience than an indication that there is a disproportionate share of tornadoes out on the plains.

There may not be much of a difference in the frequency of tornadoes on the Great Plains compared to the Midwest or Dixie Alley regions, but there are some unique characteristics of the Great Plains (Tornado Alley) tornadoes that set them apart from the rest of the country.

Unique Characteristics of Great Plains Tornadoes

The Storm Prediction Center tornado-fatality data archive for a recent thirty-year period, 1987–2016, shows us a higher incidence of tornado fatalities in Dixie Alley—Arkansas, Mississippi, and Alabama—as compared to the traditional Tornado Alley states of Oklahoma, Kansas, Nebraska, and Iowa. Using this data archive, I moved a 325-mile-by-325-mile (102,000 square miles) grid cell around the regions of Tornado Alley and Dixie Alley. The difference in tornado fatalities was dramatic.

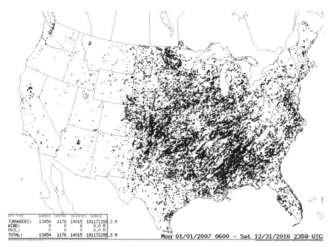

49. Observed tornadoes, all EF-Scales combined, 2007–2016, mapped using the Storm Prediction Center Severe Plot program, http://www.spc.noaa.gov/climo/online/sp3/plot.php.

For example, when this grid cell was centered on latitude 39° north, longitude 98° west (center of the traditional Tornado Alley), there was total of 2,885 tornadoes with 69 fatalities and 1,123 injuries. However, when I centered this same-sized grid cell for the same time period at latitude 33° north, longitude 89° west (center of the Dixie Alley), there were 2,276 tornadoes with 502 fatalities and 6,604 injuries. The lesson uncovered by these data is that tornadoes are far less deadly in the plains states.

The same 102,000-square-mile grid cell in Dixie Alley had 22 percent fewer tornadoes (2,276 tornadoes compared to 2,885 tornadoes) but 728 percent more fatalities (502 fatalities compared to only 69 fatalities) and 588 percent more injuries (6,604 injuries compared to 1,123 injuries). This increased fatality rate and injury rate is not the result of a higher frequency of tornadoes across these southern states, so there must be something else causing this difference.

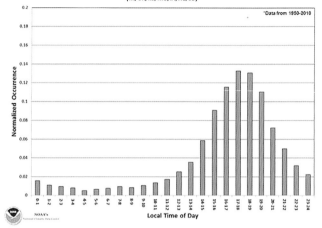

50. Tornado Alley tornadoes are highly concentrated into the late afternoon and early evening hours. Courtesy of NOAA.

Dr. Walker Ashley, a Northern Illinois University climatologist and geography professor, compiled data on killer tornadoes from 1880 to 2010 and discovered that the Mid-South has the deadliest tornadoes. "The country's most vulnerable region for tornado-related fatalities and killer tornado events basically stretches from Little Rock (Arkansas) to Memphis to Tupelo (Mississippi) to Birmingham (Alabama)," Ashley said in an NIU press release.

There are two primary factors that help explain the higher fatality rate in these states and the lower fatality rate in the Great Plains: tornado diurnal distribution and tornado seasonality. There is a stark contrast in the diurnal timing of tornadoes between the Great Plains Tornado Alley and the southeastern U.S.

In contrast to the Tornado Alley states, many of the tornadoes in the southeastern and Gulf States occur during the night (nocturnal). The percentage of nocturnal tornadoes is the highest in Tennessee with 45.8 percent of their tornadoes occurring at night. Joining Tennessee at the top of the list are Arkansas, 42.5 percent; Kentucky, 41.5 percent; and Mississippi at 39.6 percent of their tornadoes occurring at night. In contrast, Texas to Kansas averages 24 percent to 32 percent of their tornadoes at night, and Nebraska to North Dakota only 16 percent to 24 percent (see figure 50).

Only 27 percent of all tornadoes in the United States occur at night, but 39 percent of all tornado fatalities and 42 percent of killer tornado events happen at night. Ashley and two other NIU researchers determined that nighttime tornadoes—those occurring between midnight and sunrise—are 2.5 times more likely to take lives than daytime twisters. It's easy to understand that tornadoes in the middle of the night catch residents off guard and therefore are more deadly.

Since I live in Nebraska, I have archived and digitized all of the tornado records for the state. Nebraska's tornado climatology provides an excellent example of how diurnally concentrated tornadoes are on the Great Plains. A total of 2,821 tornadoes are documented for Nebraska between 1950 and 2016. A total of 56 percent of Nebraska's tornadoes have occurred during the four hours between 4:00 p.m. and 7:59 p.m. and 76 percent of Nebraska's tornadoes have occurred during the six hours between 3:00 p.m. and 8:59 p.m., with relatively few occurring after midnight. This diurnal distribution of tornadoes, standing in stark contrast to the southeastern U.S., is common throughout the plains.

Another factor keeping the Great Plains safer during tornado events is the seasonality of tornadoes. Tornadoes could happen just about any time of the year in the southeastern U.S. People can be caught off guard if tornadoes develop outside of the traditional spring season. That is, the lack of a focused tornado season may lead people to become complacent about tornado watches and warnings.

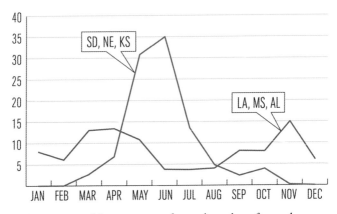

51. Average monthly percentage of annual number of tornadoes for three Great Plains states and three southeastern states, 1990–2016. Graphed by the author with data from the NOAA Storm Prediction Center.

The number of tornadoes varies significantly between the states, making it impossible to directly compare the tornado climatology of each state. The data graphed in figure 51 were standardized by converting the monthly totals into a percentage of the annual totals for each of the states being analyzed. Three Great Plains states (South Dakota, Nebraska, and Kansas) were put into the graph along with three southeastern states (Louisiana, Mississippi, and Alabama).

It is obvious that the tornado season on the Great Plains is concentrated primarily in the spring months, whereas the tornado risk is more spread out throughout the year in the southeastern states. There are also several non-meteorological factors making it safer for people experiencing tornadoes in Tornado Alley compared to Dixie Alley. For example, the Southeast has the highest percentage of mobile homes in the nation, and mobile homes are the most vulnerable structures in a tornadic situation. The southeastern U.S. also has much more forested land compared to the plains making it much more difficult to spot tornadoes there than on the open vistas of the plains.

The First Tornado Forecast Was Issued in the Great Plains

Major Fawbush and Captain Miller are also credited with making the first tornado forecast in the United States. On March 25, 1948, they issued a forecast that stated that the atmospheric conditions were primed for tornadoes in the vicinity of Tinker Air Force Base in Oklahoma. Later that same day a tornado roared through the base. Miller and Fawbush made this historic forecast with some reservation. Until March 25, 1948, tornadoes had not been forecast and many in the science community were uncertain that storms that developed so quickly and with such force could be forecast in advance.

This first tornado forecast, issued here on the Great Plains, became the first step in establishing the organized watch-and-warning system that protects the nation today. Before this time, at various stages of development of the Weather Bureau, the use of the word "tornado" in forecasts was at times strongly discouraged and at other times forbidden, because of a fear that predicting tornadoes would cause panic. This was in an era when very little was known about tornadoes compared to today, by both scientists and the public at large. In 1950 the U.S. Weather Bureau (now known as the National Weather Service) revoked the ban on mentioning tornadoes in forecasts. (The 1950 memorandum by Weather Bureau Chief F. W. Reichselder specifying this policy change can be viewed at http://www.spc .noaa.gov/faq/tornado/memo1950.pdf.)

The First Tornado Photographs Were
Taken in the Great Plains

One of the oldest known photographs of a tornado is thought to have been taken twenty-two miles southwest of Howard, South

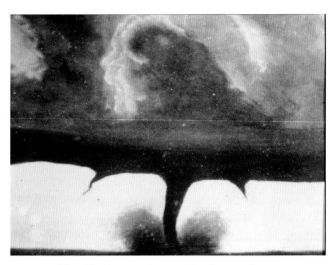

52. One of the oldest known photographs of a tornado, twenty-two miles southwest of Howard, South Dakota, August 28, 1884. It is probable however, that this image has been "altered" from the original. Image I D wea00206, N O A A's National Weather Service (N W S) Collection.

Dakota, on August 28, 1884 (see figure 52). Another tornado photograph, possibly taken just four months earlier, on April 26, 1884, is from near the small town of Garnett, Kansas. Though less dramatic than its South Dakota counterpart, the Kansas photograph, taken by A. A. Adams, who operated a photo gallery in the nearby town of Westphalia, shows a less-powerful, though well-defined tornado in the rope stage, apparently as it was dissipating near Garnett, in the heart of the Great Plains. But was the Kansas tornado photograph really the earliest? While meteorologists and historians are still debating the accuracy of the dates of these two photographs, they do agree that the two photos, using an emerging technology of photography, undoubtedly paved the way for the many storm chasers who would follow, crisscrossing the plains in search of the "ideal" tornado photograph.

Most Active Tornado Area within the Great Plains

The epicenter of highest tornado frequency in the Great Plains can be found in the Oklahoma City vicinity. The relatively small community of Moore, Oklahoma, a suburb on the south side of Oklahoma City, has been hit by eight tornadoes in just the last eighteen years alone. There are several examples of residents completely losing their house in Moore, rebuilding, and then losing their home again just a few years later. There have been an incredible 156 tornadoes that have occurred wholly or partly within the Oklahoma City boundaries between 1890 and 2013 (see figure 53).

With this impressive density of tornado occurrences, it is no coincidence that the National Severe Storms Laboratory (NSSL) and the National Weather Service's Storm Prediction Center (SPC) are both located in Norman, Oklahoma, just to the south of this tornado occurrence epicenter.

The Great Plains Is Home to the Largest U.S. Tornadoes

On May 31, 2013, a deadly, multiple-vortex tornado near El Reno, Oklahoma, carved an official maximum path width of 2.6 miles, based on damage and some radar estimates. That width barely exceeded the 2.5 miles of the Hallam, Nebraska, EF-4 tornado of May 22, 2004. El Reno and Hallam probably were close to the maximum size for tornadoes; but it is quite possible that others this size or somewhat larger have occurred that weren't sampled by high-resolution radar or surveyed so carefully in the field. It is interesting to note that the costliest U.S. tornado also occurred in the Great Plains as noted below.

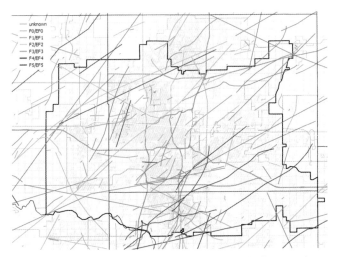

53. Tracks of all 156 recorded tornadoes occurring wholly or partly within the immediate Oklahoma City, Oklahoma, area, 1890–2013. County boundaries and major highways are shown. Maps courtesy of the National Weather Service at Norman, Oklahoma, https://www.weather.gov/oun/tornadodata-okc-figure5.

Historical Tornadoes in the Great Plains

Despite it being, in general, safer in the Great Plains during tornadoes, some of the deadliest U.S. tornadoes have occurred in the Great Plains. Here are the top five.

1. **Woodward, Oklahoma, April 9, 1947**

   The "Woodward Tornado" wreaked havoc across parts of Texas, Oklahoma, and Kansas on April 9, 1947, killing 181 people and injuring 970. The funnel cloud reportedly was more than a mile wide in places.

2. **Joplin, Missouri, May 22, 2011**

   The EF-5 tornado that struck Joplin on May 22, 2011, killed 158 people and injured more than 1,000. The storm packed winds in excess of 200 mph and was on the ground for more than twenty-two miles. This EF-5 in Joplin was the costliest tornado on record, with an estimated $2.8 billion in damage (in 2011 dollars).

3. Waco, Texas, May 11, 1953

On May 11, 1953, an EF-5 tornado cut a path nearly one-third of a mile wide through Waco, injuring 600 people, causing 114 fatalities, and destroying hundreds of businesses. Around 4:30 p.m. the tornado touched down southwest of Waco and tore through residential areas. By 4:36 p.m., it struck downtown Waco. Many of the buildings in downtown Waco were not built to withstand the destructive power of a tornado. Only buildings with steel-frame structures, such as the Amicable Building and the Roosevelt Hotel, were able to withstand the severe winds. Others, such as the R. T. Dennis Building, collapsed, killing thirty of the people within and injuring several more. The tornado destroyed 196 buildings, and damaged hundreds of others so badly that they were later torn down. Though estimates vary, approximately $51 million (in 1953 dollars) in property damages occurred. Although this catastrophe—recognized as the deadliest Texas tornado since 1900—devastated downtown Waco, it was also one of the contributing factors for the emergence of an efficient tornado warning system for the entire nation.

4. Goliad, Texas, 1902

The Goliad tornado of 1902 is ranked as the fourth-deadliest tornado in the Great Plains. There is a historical marker noting this event in Goliad:

> "A cyclone, considered one of the two most disastrous in Texas history, struck Goliad on Sunday, May 18, 1902.

The twister touched down on the south side of the San Antonio River at 3:35 p.m. Sounding like a heavily loaded freight train, the storm ripped a mile long, half-mile-wide path across the northwest section of town, destroying over 100 homes and leaving an official death toll of 114. At least fifty members of a black Methodist church died when their sanctuary was razed. After the disaster, the Goliad County courthouse served as a temporary hospital and morgue."

As noted earlier, the people of this time had none of today's instant access to weather information or any form of advance warnings.

5. Omaha, Nebraska, March 23, 1913

Imagine what it was like compared to today, with all of our social media and news media keeping us informed of developing severe weather. This tornado tore through the city without any advance warning. A total of 103 people died in this storm. According to the newspaper reports at the time, the tornado was so strong that steel train cars were later found pierced by pieces of debris from destroyed houses.

Three Memorable Tornadoes on the Plains

Since moving to the Great Plains, I can recount three tornadoes that were the most memorable for me. My first year living in Nebraska saw the January 10–11, 1975, eastern Nebraska blizzard and then the powerful tornado that tore through Omaha on May 6, 1975. What a dramatic introduction to extreme weather on the plains. Of the three tornado events in Nebraska that have had the greatest impact on me, the first two had me conducting damage surveys the morning following the tornadoes, and I was involved in the third as a storm chaser and observer of the tornado as well as participating in the damage survey.

Omaha, Nebraska, May 6, 1975

An outbreak of several large and powerful tornadoes occurred in eastern Nebraska on May 5, 1975. One of these tornadoes entered the southern part of Omaha and then traveled through the city along one of the busiest corridors right at the start of rush hour. There was no internet, or Weather Radio or Weather Channel television station from which to get updates on the developing severe weather in 1975, so I had to get my information from a local radio station in Lincoln.

From this station I learned that the National Weather Service Severe Storms Forecast Center (then in Kansas City, Missouri) had issued, shortly after 12:30 p.m., a tornado watch for eastern Nebraska, valid from 2:00 p.m. to 8:00 p.m. on that day. I went outside and it felt like a sauna with very high humidity, the sun blazing down on me and temperatures pushing toward 80°. The sky was a hazy, milky-white color due to the large amount of water vapor in the atmosphere. Strong southeast winds all day had been pumping up Gulf moisture into southeastern Nebraska.

Scattered puffy cumulus clouds had been forming for several hours but now several of them had begun to suddenly tower and "boil" upward just off to the east of Lincoln. I could hear a few rumbles of thunder off in the distance. It was very obvious to me that several of these thunderstorms to the east of Lincoln were turning into dangerous monsters capable of producing tornadoes.

Suddenly the wind shifted at my location in Lincoln and was coming out of the southwest behind what is called a "dry line." This desertlike air pushed the clouds rapidly off to the northeast and the clear dry air changed the sky from a hazy, white, humid sky to a bright blue color. Relative humidity that had been in the 65 percent range dropped to just below 10 percent. It no longer felt like I was living in the Gulf Coast region of the U.S. but, instead, like I was standing in the Arizona desert. Although most people think that moist air is denser than dry air, just the opposite is in fact the case. While there are more water vapor molecules in moist air than dry air, these molecules are themselves lighter than the molecules of nitrogen and oxygen (and trace amounts of other gases) that are also present. These somewhat heavier gases, however, still have to make room for the water vapor molecules, resulting in the air molecules being pushed further apart and thus resulting in reduced air density. We can see, then, that the dry air pushing into Nebraska from the southwest that afternoon was denser than moist air, and it was slamming into the storms that were rapidly growing between Lincoln and Omaha. The storms rose up over seventy thousand feet above the surface as they approached Omaha. The distance between the eastern edge of Lincoln and the western edge of Omaha is only forty-five miles, so I was able to see these thunderstorms towering up over the plains. I instinctively knew that Omaha would soon be hit with some monster thunderstorms.

Shortly after 2:00 p.m., the Omaha National Weather Service office issued a severe thunderstorm warning for several counties based upon radar data. They reissued the warning again at 3:15 p.m., based on storm-spotter reports of damaging wind and hail to the south and southwest of Omaha. Storm spotters at 4:09 p.m. observed a tornado in Sarpy County and the county activated the warning sirens. Shortly after 4:14 p.m., a tornado warning was issued for Omaha and the three-county area. The tornado slammed into the apartments at Ninety-sixth and Q Streets at 4:33 p.m. and continued northeast, approaching I-80 near Eighty-Fourth Street. As it crossed I-80, it tossed cars off the road and into the ditches along the interstate, resulting in numerous injuries. The tornado continued moving north shifting slightly to the east to travel right up the Seventy-Second Street business corridor. At 4:58 p.m. the tornado lifted and dissipated over Benson Park.

The damage path was ten miles in length and at some points a quarter-mile wide. Damage estimates at the time ranged from $250 million to $500 million (in 1975 dollars). The number of homes totally destroyed was 287, with damage to 1,400 others. There were 110 documented injuries, but there were many more that were minor and didn't get documented at the time. The Omaha NWS estimated that there were between two hundred and three hundred injuries from the tornado. Three people did perish: an elderly woman died in her home and likely did not hear the warnings; a waitress was killed in a restaurant as she huddled with others in the restroom; and a man was killed while seeking shelter at a gas station. The death toll could have been much higher were it not for the fact that this tornado occurred during daylight so that it could be seen approaching Omaha and, along with hearing the warning sirens, people could seek shelter.

The national and local news reports the next morning described and showed some of the devastation that had been caused by this tornado. Prior to this tornado, the last time that I had seen this much damage from a strong tornado was in Oak Lawn, Illinois (suburban Chicago) in 1967. Although I had no family connection to the Omaha tornado, after watching the morning news, I was emotionally fixated on going to see the damage. I stopped by my office on the UNL campus, picked up one of my graduate students, and we drove to Omaha on I-80. As we approached Eighty-Fourth Street from the west, it was a surreal scene, with tow trucks pulling damaged cars out of the ditches lining the interstate. The Nebraska State Patrol was there making sure no one stopped to take photos or interfere with the recovery efforts. Looking to the left and north of I-80, we could see that houses had been ripped apart. As we approached the Seventy-Second Street exit, we were back to normalcy with no damage in the immediate vicinity. We drove one block north on Seventy-Second Street and pulled into a blocked-off side road just to the west. I spoke briefly with law enforcement that had the area secured to prevent sightseers from entering while recovery efforts were underway. I explained that I was a UNL geography professor and I was there to photograph and map the damage for research and educational purposes. We were given permission to enter the closed-off area and ordered to "stay out of the way" of the recovery efforts. We walked several blocks west and then headed back south to the houses backing up to the north side of I-80.

We walked up to a house located immediately north of I-80 that had no roof or walls. We visited with the news crew that had arrived at the same time that we did, and I listened in on the interview with the resident of that house. She explained to the news reporter that she left immediately after the tornado destroyed her house and that she had only just now returned to see what it looked like. She pointed out that the dining-room table had been set for dinner just before the tornado hit and she hadn't noticed when she'd left the house after the tornado that the dishes and glasses were untouched. Somehow the tornado took off the roof, carried away the walls, but left the dinner table untouched.

As we walked north along the western edge of the tornado-damaged area, I stopped at a home that was not only destroyed, but the contents of the basement, including the furnace, had also been ripped out of the house. As I stood in the backyard, photographing the damaged house, I looked across the street and there was absolutely no damage. The tornado had sliced surgically through the neighborhood with homes totally destroyed immediately across the street from homes with no damage at all. What made it an even stranger scene was the man across the street loading fertilizer into his lawn spreader and doing yard work as if nothing had ever happened; and for him, nothing *had* happened to him and his house when the storm roared through his neighborhood.

We spent the day wandering through the damage path, taking photos and doing our best to stay away from the heavy machinery that had been brought in to remove debris from the damaged homes and businesses. Occasionally people would approach us and share their story of what it was like to have lived through the tornado. I was so impressed with the way the people at work and at home in the damage path of the tornado had done exactly what they needed to do to survive the storm. When you watch news coverage of a disaster, the news media usually seeks out and features people who are emotionally distraught and very upset. It was the opposite experience for us, with every person that we met having a positive attitude. So many times we heard variations of "We still have each other; all we lost was stuff and that can be replaced." It was refreshing to see the resilient nature of Nebraskans, a trait that I have seen all across the Great Plains.

I learned a lot that day about tornado damage and storm safety. The photos that I took on that day became the first set of illustrations that I would use in my public talks about storm safety and in my classroom lectures. When I returned home that evening, I sat on the front porch, tired and somewhat pensive, thinking about what I had seen that day and almost feeling guilty that I could return to my home and possessions when so many people had lost their homes in Omaha. After seeing the damage from the Oak Lawn, Illinois, tornado of April 21, 1967, and the Omaha May 6, 1975, tornado, I knew that I wanted to focus my career and public educational outreach in the areas of storm survival and storm-loss mitigation. And this is what I have achieved by being on the Chancellor's Speakers Bureau giving public talks for many years, along with my annual spring Weatherfest, my "weather in the classroom" school visits, and my weather and climate websites at the University of Nebraska–Lincoln.

Grand Island, Nebraska, June 3, 1980

June 3, 1980, was a cloudless, sunny day across Nebraska with strong southerly winds pumping up moisture and heat across the Great Plains. Nebraska, and much of the Great Plains, was under what is called a "heat ridge," which would normally suppress any thunderstorm development. Typically, in this type of a situation, scattered cumulus clouds develop in the late afternoon but as they grow vertically they hit what is termed a "cap," which is another way of saying that descending warm air in the heat ridge "caps," or stops, any robust vertical development. Somehow, against all odds, a weak spot in the "cap" existed over central Nebraska that day and a cumulus cloud found an open access to higher elevation, causing it to explode upward to over sixty-five thousand feet above sea level just north of Grand Island. There was so much energy flowing up into that single thunderstorm that it overshot the top of the storm and spread out into the clouds that were forming the shape of an anvil out ahead of the thunderstorm. The anvil reached not only Lincoln, by sunset, but later in the evening while the thunderstorm remained on top of Grand Island, the anvil cloud reached all the way to Des Moines, Iowa.

This massive thunderstorm, also termed a "supercell," moved slowly south-southeast through the city at around eight mph. At approximately 8:45 p.m., the first of seven tornadoes touched down eleven miles northwest of Grand Island. The seven-hundred-yard-wide F-3 tornado tracked south for seven miles,

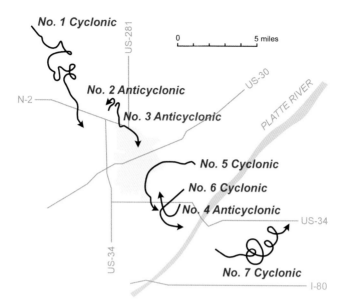

No. 1 Cyclonic

US-281

0   5 miles

US-30

PLATTE RIVER

N-2

No. 2 Anticyclonic

No. 3 Anticyclonic

No. 5 Cyclonic

No. 6 Cyclonic

No. 4 Anticyclonic

US-34

US-34

No. 7 Cyclonic

I-80

54. Grand Island tornadoes, June 3, 1980. Map created by Dee
Ebbeka with data acquired from Dr. Roger Wakimoto.

ending four miles northwest of downtown Grand Island (see
figure 54). While the straight-line path was seven miles, the
twisting and erratic movement covered over twice that distance,
at just over fourteen miles, while spending forty-nine minutes
on the ground.

The last of the seven tornadoes touched down at 10:45 p.m.,
and just like the first tornado of the evening, it took a very
erratic, looping path. It finally lifted and dissipated at 11:30
p.m., two hours and forty-five minutes after the first of the seven
tornadoes developed. In addition to these seven tornadoes, the
city was slammed with downburst winds from the thunderstorm,
producing extensive damage in the Capital Heights area of
northwest Grand Island and near the slow-moving looping
tornado (number 7 on the map in figure 54). There were two

unusual aspects of the Grand Island tornadoes: first, a single thunderstorm produced seven tornadoes in the same vicinity and, secondly, three of the tornadoes rotated anticyclonically, or clockwise, a rare occasion in the Northern Hemisphere, where almost all tornadoes rotate cyclonically, or counterclockwise.

Five people were killed and about two hundred were injured; 475 living units and forty-nine businesses were totally destroyed, with a total damage of nearly $300 million (in 1980 dollars). The book and movie both titled *The Night of the Twisters* is based on these seven Grand Island tornadoes of June 3.

I wasn't expecting any severe weather on this day, and as I headed out midevening to run some errands in Lincoln, I was surprised to see a huge thunderstorm anvil off to the west. I remember watching the local 10:00 p.m. news and weather broadcast that evening in Lincoln. The newscaster reported that damaging tornadoes had struck Grand Island and that tornadoes continued to form and plow through the city. It was also reported that the National Weather Service office as well as the air traffic control tower, both located at the Grand Island Airport, had to be abandoned when a tornado approached the airport. This was verified when I visited the Grand Island National Weather Service office later in the week. The fifteen-mile-high thunderstorm, which had remained in place for hours, suddenly collapsed after the last of the seven tornadoes lifted and dissipated. There was a tremendous outward rush of air when this occurred. Imagine a fifteen-mile-high dam holding back water and then the dam collapses, water rushing out in a huge wave, and you can imagine the amount of air that came out of that thunderstorm when it collapsed. Just after midnight this "wave" of air slammed into Lincoln shaking our house for several minutes and then it was all calm.

The national television news broadcast from New York City the next morning, in an exaggerated statement, reported that tornadoes had wiped Grand Island off the map. I packed a cooler with ice and drinks and several sandwiches, drove to the UNL city campus, and stopped by my office to pick up a few things before heading out to Grand Island. My phone was ringing as I opened my office door; it was an administrative secretary at Texas Tech University. I was asked to reserve a private plane at Duncan Aviation, at the Lincoln airport, for Dr. James McDonald, of the National Wind Institute, who was already on the way to Lincoln on a commercial aircraft along with several of his research colleagues.

The study of wind at Texas Tech began in 1970, following an F-5 tornado in Lubbock that caused twenty-six fatalities and more than $100 million in damages. Since that time, Texas Tech's commitment to wind research has evolved into the National Wind Institute, a collaborative, interdisciplinary institute that involves atmospheric science, economics, mathematics, civil, mechanical, and electrical engineering, construction engineering, computer science, sociology, law, and business. As part of their mission back then, as well as now, they have several large research projects focused on wind hazard mitigation and other aspects of wind science and engineering. McDonald and his colleagues wanted to do a ground survey as well as an aerial survey of the Grand Island tornado damage.

Reserving the plane was one of the strangest tasks that I had in my entire career. After going to the Duncan Aviation facility at the Lincoln airport, I told them what we needed, picked out a plane, and they assigned a private pilot to the aircraft. I remember just standing there with a big grin on my face thinking, "It's not every day you get to book an entire plane. I have a pretty cool job." I then headed over to the commercial part of the airport to wait for Dr. McDonald and his colleagues and then brought them to their waiting private plane. They told me that the Grand Island tornado event was very unusual and they encouraged me to go there to conduct my own survey of the damage.

I immediately went back to my office and invited one of my colleagues to join me in going out to Grand Island to do a damage survey. I have had an amateur radio license since I was in high school, and the local Lincoln Amateur Radio Club was providing communications between Lincoln and Grand Island as well as bringing in supplies to the emergency management agency looking after the recovery efforts in Grand Island. Using my amateur radio to communicate with the command center, I was guided into Stolley Park Elementary School, about six blocks west of the largest damage corridor. I received a quick briefing, looked at their large map of Grand Island, where they were outlining the damage areas, and realized Grand Island had been struck by multiple tornadoes.

I started the photographic damage survey in the southeastern edge of Grand Island and circumnavigated the city finding damage in multiple areas. We then decided to focus on the largest and most damaging tornado, the F-4 tornado that came in from the east along Bismark Road and then turned south, going right down the center of the main business corridor on Locust Street. There are so many stories and experiences from that day that remain engraved in my memory.

Our first stop was at the Mavis Bowling Alley, on Bismark Road and at the east edge of Grand Island. We entered the building and found no roof over the lanes. Two cars had been lofted into the bowling alley and were lying on their sides on lanes one and four. Just like the house that I saw in Omaha following their May 1975 tornado, where the dinner table was untouched but the walls and roof were gone, the cup holders still had drinks in them and cigarettes were still in ashtrays, all untouched, yet the bowling alley had been destroyed by the tornado. We met the bartender, who related in detail what it was like to be in the building as the tornado approached and how he herded the staff and customers into the cooler where it went dark moments later when the electricity went out. All they could hear was, as he described it, "the bowling alley being put into a blender." No one was hurt since they took shelter in the strongest part of the building. He told us that after it got totally quiet, they forced the cooler door open and stepped out into the remains of the bowling alley and a world torn apart.

The first emergency management vehicles and residents that attempted to drive into the tornado-damaged areas got flat tires on their vehicles as they drove over boards with exposed nails. We were given information about which streets were cleared of all debris so that we could safely navigate the damage areas. Not too far from the bowling alley, there was a street that ended in a cu-de-sac, with a small green space in the middle of the street with some trees and bushes. What immediately caught our eye was that most of the cars in this street were swept off the driveways and swirled together and then dumped in the middle of the circle almost like a deliberate, albeit odd, sculpture. A few days later this was the spot where President Jimmy Carter met with the media and announced federal assistance for the city. We got out of the car and took some photos there and in the surrounding neighborhood.

When we returned to the car, I put the tailgate of my station wagon down and the two of us took a break to have a can of soda from the cooler and to eat our lunches that we'd brought from Lincoln. We were sitting on the tailgate, oblivious to our surroundings and laughing over some story that we shared that I can no longer remember. What I do recall vividly is that our laughter abruptly ended when a man appeared out of nowhere, hot, sweaty, and dirty. He stood directly in front of us. In a very emotionless tone he asked, "Could I buy a soda from your cooler?" I immediately said "No . . ." He began to slowly walk away when I realized he hadn't heard the rest of the sentence which was "No, but you can have as many as you want for free." His face showed incredible sadness and I quickly yelled, "Come back! I said no, you don't have to pay for them." He stood there in silence for a moment and then said thanks and then looked straight at us and said, "You have no idea," and walked away. That encounter still haunts me today.

We followed the damage path west to the main north-south corridor, Locust Street. Along the way, we noticed that the tornado had skirted the edge of the Grand Island Fonner Park race track just like the Omaha 1975 tornado had skirted the edge of the Aksarben race track. We knew there was no cause and effect, but we found the coincidence interesting and amusing. We parked just off Locust Street to do the survey of the damage path of the strongest and widest of the seven Grand Island tornadoes. We spent over four hours walking through this area.

A little over a year later, the Omaha local chapter of the American Meteorological Society invited Dr. Ted Fujita (the scientist for whom the F-Scale is named) to give a public talk about the Grand Island tornadoes. He and his graduate student, Roger Wakimoto, had spent several days walking along each of the tornado-damage paths doing an exhaustive ground survey of all of the damage. The map shown in figure 54, of the Grand Island tornadoes, was produced by Roger Wakimoto following their survey. Dr. Fujita stressed that the Grand Island event was very unusual and that we would likely learn more about tornadoes from this one event than any other tornado event in our data archives.

He also talked about the dangers of downburst winds and showed a series of photos from the Capital Heights area in northwest Grand Island. He repeated multiple times, "Garage door up, big problem, garage door down, no problem," as he clicked through the photos. He proved that when the 100-mph wind gusts burst out of the thunderstorm, if the garage door was up, air rushed into the garage lifting the house structure and partially destroying it. If the garage door was down when the downburst hit, only minor structural damage occurred. I included this observation in all of my subsequent public tornado-safety talks: a house will better survive strong winds if all of the windows and doors are closed tight. I also began to use this Grand Island tornado-damage evidence to dispel the quickly growing myth that a house would better withstand a direct hit by a tornado if the windows were opened so that the difference in air pressure could be equalized. My colleagues and I do not know where that misconception originated, but we still hear the public repeating that myth on occasion and we easily and quickly dispel it with what we learned in the Grand Island tornadoes of 1980.

Hallam, Nebraska, June 22, 2004

It was a typical early-summer day across Nebraska with warm temperatures and clear skies. Most residents didn't know about the potential for severe weather on this day, but my storm chase team did. Our University of Nebraska student storm chase team met at my house early in the morning of June 22, 2004, to discuss our plans for the day (see figure 55). Two Weather Channel forecasters who were longtime friends of mine were staying at my house and joined us that day for our storm chase across Nebraska.

Our ability to storm chase by 2004 had greatly improved with access to cell phones in the car and wireless hotspots to access the internet forecast products with our laptop computers. We also had access to weather radar in our cars at this time using a system called Threat Net, which used the same type of antenna used for today's satellite radios in cars. When I first

55. Author's storm chase team, along with other storm chase colleagues, gathers at my house to review the forecast information on the internet and plan our storm chase plans for the day, May 22, 2004. Photo by the author.

started storm chasing two decades earlier, all I could do was aim toward where we thought storms would form and observe the weather around us, but by 2004 we were able to readjust our targets as the storm chases unfolded.

There was no doubt in our minds that this was going to be a very active severe-weather day with the potential for numerous tornadoes east of a line between I-80 at Lexington, Nebraska, and the Kansas border. As I left with the group to get into our three vehicles I turned to my wife and said, "I hope I don't see you this afternoon." I knew what I meant, but apparently my students didn't. One of the students who felt comfortable asking me, whispered, "Why did you not want to see your wife this afternoon?" I quickly responded, "Because if I do, that would mean there would be tornadoes in Lincoln and headed toward my house." Little did I know at the time that this was actually a strong possibility.

We headed west on I-80 and found a WiFi hotspot in Kearney, where we accessed our laptop computers to review the latest online forecast guidance. My Weather Channel colleagues who were with our group got on their cell phone and began a day-long series of live updates for the Weather Channel back in Atlanta, Georgia. We were in exactly the right spot as a thunderstorm twenty miles to our southwest began to explode upward and it quickly generated our first tornado intercept of the day. The NOAA Storm Prediction Center data archive shows a total of eighty-six reported tornadoes reported on this day with over sixty tornado reports in Nebraska. The Nebraska tornadoes all occurred between the I-80 corridor and the Kansas border beginning just after 5:00 p.m. and ending just a few minutes before midnight. This was a record number of tornadoes for a single day in Nebraska and was the contributing factor for a record number of tornadoes in the month of May (76) and in a single year (110). Both records remain unbroken as of 2017.

I rarely take a photo of myself in front of a tornado, but on this day I did because I had the feeling that this was going to be a historic outbreak of tornadoes across the state. The few times that I have been photographed in front of a tornado, I have never smiled or shouted with excitement for I long ago learned that these atmospheric monsters can bring heartache and tragedy (see figures 56 and 57).

We drove behind the thunderstorms as they, one after another, became violent and produced tornadoes. As the afternoon progressed into early evening, the thunderstorms became heavy rain producers and the tornadoes would play "hide and seek" with us as curtains of rain would wrap around the funnels obscuring them from view. This made it very dangerous for us as storm chasers since we weren't always sure if the thunderstorm that

56. The first tornado intercept of the day with a member of our storm chase team and the navigator in my car communicating with the National Weather Service about the location of the tornado. Photo by the author.

57. Another tornado intercept on May 22, 2004. Photo by the author.

we were following at any given time was just a rain producer or hiding a tornado inside the rain curtain.

Much of that afternoon is a blur in my memory since we cut back and forth across the county roads dodging the hail portions of the thunderstorms and catching the occasional glimpses of tornadoes. It was surreal in many ways and reminded me of the movie *Twister*; except that we weren't watching the movie, we were instead now in our own version of the movie. We would occasionally encounter other storm chasers who were friends, yet there was no time to visit, so we would just roll down our vehicle windows and yell, "Hi, good to see you. Stay safe." It was starting to get dark as sunset was rapidly approaching and we found ourselves heading toward a storm that was growing larger and larger and actually emitting a growling sound with continuous rolling thunder.

It was obvious to us that this was no ordinary thunderstorm. It seemed like it kept growing and growing and producing almost constant thunder. The sky near the storm turned a shade of green that is typical of a highly electrically charged thunderstorm and one that is producing a large volume of hail. We did not feel comfortable getting any closer than we were, and we felt better knowing that it was moving away from us. In all of my many years of chasing storms, this was only the second storm I encountered that actually sounded like it was growling. We called it "the beast" and made sure we kept a healthy distance from it.

It was getting too dark at this time to do any more photography, and it wouldn't be safe to be stopped on the side of the road. We decided to travel as a group and stay together, communicating between vehicles using our handheld radios. Several newly developed tornado-warned storms were in our way if we were to go north, so our only way back to Lincoln was to head east behind this storm using gravel-and-dirt county roads.

Although we couldn't see the tornado that was eventually going to slam into Hallam, we began to see damage as we traversed these rural roads. Sometimes wires were down on the road or trees were blocking our way and we had to turn around and find another county road. At one point, we turned around in a farmyard and the headlights of our car suddenly illuminated a farmhouse that had been badly damaged. There were some people outside and they yelled that they were okay.

It was very quiet in my vehicle and I learned later it was also very quiet in the other vehicles of our storm chase team. It was totally dark at this point and we continued to find tornado damage and debris forcing us to choose another gravel road. At one point we found ourselves on a dirt road and, as any Nebraskan would know, our clay soil when wet is as slippery as ice. The lead car in our caravan had trouble making it to the top of small hill and it kept sliding backward. Finally we all backed up and tried a different unmarked county road. We did not know at the time, but the storm that we photographed earlier had become even larger and had a massive tornado that was getting dangerously close to us.

We were at the northwestern edge of the thunderstorm that was producing the Hallam tornado and although we were not in danger, we all felt very apprehensive. We were pleased that the storm was quickly moving away and we could again proceed toward Lincoln. The storm chase navigator in the lead car said we should hold back a few more minutes to put lots of space between us and the storm. I looked at my cell phone and saw that I actually had a signal from a cell tower so I decided to call home. The phone rang many times and, just as it went to the answering machine, my wife answered the phone. I asked her why it took her so long to get to the phone and she said that she had been downstairs in the basement safe room since there was a tornado warning in Lincoln and the sirens were blaring. Our home at the time was on the very southeast edge of Lincoln near Nebraska Highway 2. She commented that there were occasional loud thumps outside the house and she didn't know what it was. I quickly sent her back downstairs, turned off the cell phone and realized that the Hallam tornado was likely headed in her direction. The sirens had been turned on in Lincoln because the initial path of the Hallam tornado was taking it up right through the center of the city. As the tornado moved northeast it began to shift ever so slightly to the east and missed Lincoln, but only by a few miles. The noises that she heard were from debris being ejected from the Hallam tornado as the tornado approached Highway 2, just a few miles to the east of our home. The next day we found two-by-four lumber tornado debris impaled in our lawn as well as in a nearby golf course.

The noise of chatter picked up quickly in my car with a collective sigh of relief as we turned on the headlights and drove east several miles to a paved road, Nebraska Highway 77, which heads north up to Lincoln. At this point, we did not know what had happened in Hallam. All we knew was that an extremely large thunderstorm with a rain-wrapped tornado had moved through the area and that we had crossed the damage path several times while trying to get back to Lincoln. As we pulled away from the stop sign and began to head north to Lincoln it became very quiet again as we watched a wall of flashing red lights (fire engines, ambulances, state patrol cars) rapidly heading south on the other side of the road. We didn't know what had happened, but we knew something dreadful must have occurred. The lights of Lincoln were soon visible ahead and we drove across the far southern edge of Lincoln, arriving at my home with the front door open and the T V loudly playing in the family room.

My U N L storm chase team and my Weather Channel colleagues with us that day were physically exhausted and emotionally drained as we gathered inside my house. However, we were jolted wide awake as we began to mentally take in the live TV news report that Hallam had been destroyed by a tornado. I picked up the phone, went to another room in the house, and called the KLKN-TV studio and asked the person answering the phone to write down my name and hand it to Kevin Coskren, even if he is on the air. Suddenly, I hear his voice coming out of the family room TV saying, "We have Ken Dewey on the phone and I know he was out there today with his storm chase team. Ken, tell us what you know and what did you see today." I remained on the phone for the next thirty minutes and Kevin would give news updates and then turn it back to me as I described our day and what we had seen across the state, as well as our encounter with the edge of the Hallam tornado and the scene of all the emergency management vehicles headed toward Hallam. I stepped back into the family room briefly and the TV was now on the Weather Channel and my storm chase friend, Weather Channel forecaster Matt Crowther, was sitting on my couch reporting live, via his phone, to the Weather Channel in Atlanta, Georgia.

There was absolutely no way I was going to sleep after this dramatic storm chase day. Instead, I stayed up and was looking at various internet weather-related websites. The quiet of my house was suddenly interrupted with my cell phone ringing. It was one of the students from our storm chase team and he was obviously very troubled by our close encounter with the Hallam tornado and wanted to talk about it. We didn't know at the time, but this monster tornado was a record two and a half miles wide. He wanted to know if he, and whoever else wanted to join us, could trace our path in daylight to see how close we had been to the path of the Hallam tornado. He directed me to the NOAA Storm Prediction Center website, which archives all of the tornado storm reports in near real time. I read out loud the Lancaster County Emergency Management report that was submitted to the National Weather Service in Omaha and relayed to the SPC earlier in the evening at 8:35 p.m.: "Houses destroyed and power lines down. Requesting a lot of help. Medical call requested to Hallam, Nebraska, as major damage has occurred."

The next morning, just after sunrise, I went to the Lancaster County Emergency Operations Command Center and met with their director, Doug Ahlberg. I had worked with Doug for over a decade, providing student meteorology interns to help with the forecasting of extreme weather events. I had also organized and hosted the annual county storm-spotter training workshops each spring at the UNL Weatherfest and Central Plains Severe Weather Symposium. Doug greeted me with, "It's real this time and it's bad." We headed down to Hallam to survey the damage and check on the efforts to get the town accessible to its returning residents. All of the residents had been transported by bus to Lincoln soon after the tornado struck their town. Several law enforcement agencies were at the perimeter of the town to keep sightseers out of the area. We needed to make sure that the streets were safe to walk on, and that there were no hazards, like live power lines, before residents would be allowed to return to what was left of their homes.

I had visited many tornado-damaged areas in the past and had always gotten permission after I showed an ID to law enforcement and explained why I wanted to be there to photograph the damage. This was the first time that as I approached the security perimeter of a tornado-damaged community, the security officials looked up at me and just waved me in. Yes, these were the very people that I had gotten to know over the years in our storm-spotter training workshops. One of them called my name as I walked into the secure area and said, "Well it finally happened right here in our backyard" (meaning near Lincoln).

58. This house was picked up by the May 22, 2004, tornado, spun around, and dropped on its side, spilling out all of its contents and creating the appearance of "cornucopia." Photo by the author.

I walked up and down each of the streets in this small community, taking photos. The streets had debris moved to the side but all of the structures were still untouched by any of the residents or by heavy machinery. This allowed me to once again get a close look at how buildings fail during tornado events. By midafternoon the all-clear was issued to allow residents back into town after they identified themselves at the security checkpoints. At this point I only took a few more photos as the residents began to return to their homes. I have never felt comfortable taking photos of people in disasters, feeling like I was intruding on their personal space and not allowing their privacy to deal with their emotions. However, on this first day after the tornado and the days that I returned over the next two weeks to document the recovery efforts, some of the residents approached me and wanted to tell their stories about their encounter with this beast of a storm.

59. Norris High School auditorium, just a few miles northwest of Hallam, Nebraska, after the May 22, 2004, tornado. Note the red seats buried under debris; this is why large open rooms with side-span roofs should be avoided in tornado situations. This would include auditoriums, gymnasiums, and any of the so-called big-box stores. Photo by the author.

The couple seen in figure 58 came over to tell me about their experience. The woman had been at home during the tornado and rode out the storm in a small cellar as their house was lofted into the air, spun around, and slammed back down to the ground. They expressed no anger and, after a pleasant chat, said they needed to get back to getting what they could out of the house.

I surveyed the damage both in Hallam and along the path in the rural areas both to the west and east of Hallam. The Norris High School damage was shocking and some of the most extreme damage that I have ever seen for school buildings (see figure 59).

60. Staged photo of Ryan McGinnis, the author, and Carrie Wood Cunningham while storm chasing in the Great Plains in June 2010. Photo by Gino De Grandis.

And finally, I end this chapter with some irony: The Day the Storms Chased the Storm Chaser.

On the afternoon of May 9, 2016, I was at home working on this book and describing my first encounter with a tornado in Chicago. As I noted in chapter 1, the March 1961 Chicago tornado happened very suddenly and without any awareness on my part that a tornado was even possible, and it came within a few miles of my house. It was about to happen again.

Figure 60 shows a staged photo of Ryan McGinnis, Carrie Wood Cunningham, and me taken by our friend Gino De Grandis when the four of us were out storm chasing on the Great Plains in June 2010. Although the intent was just to take a fun photo of us out storm chasing on the plains, the photo encapsulates my encounter with my first tornado back in Chicago in 1961 and then again with the tornado that approached my house on May 9, 2016.

My house windows were open and it was sunny with just a few puffy cumulus clouds during the afternoon of May 9, 2016. I actually was not paying much attention to the weather forecast or the latest weather satellite or radar data. As I was entering text into the computer in my home office, thunder suddenly boomed throughout my neighborhood and a dark cloud obscured the warm spring sunshine. I stepped out onto the front porch and it was obvious that a thunderstorm had suddenly formed and was explosively growing over southeast Lincoln. I was caught off guard since I had been focused on doing research and writing and hadn't paid any attention to the weather conditions for several hours. This time no one ordered me to take my enthusiasm upstairs, and I decided on my own to go up to the top floor of the house where I might have a better view of the developing storm. And just like so many years ago when I saw my first tornado in Chicago, a tornado formed in front of me and dropped down from the clouds within several miles of my house.

My enthusiasm and excitement this time was channeled into social media where I began to provide updates about the storm from its very beginning, to the formation of the tornado, and then the one-hour hailstorm that battered my house and neighborhood. Rusty Dawkins, my former student and KOLN/KGIN television weathercaster, and I began to push the tornado information out to the public on our individual Twitter accounts and retweeted each other's posts as well.

While I shot video from the top floor of my house, my neighbor and colleague, Bill Sorensen, living across the street from me, took the photo of the tornado seen in figure 61 from ground level as it approached our neighborhood. The tornado was approximately two miles from my house at this time.

KMTV, an ABC-TV affiliate in Omaha, had been following my social media postings throughout the storm and sent a

61. Tornado photo taken near the author's house, May 9, 2016. Photo by Bill Sorensen.

news crew into my neighborhood after the storm ended. They contacted me to do a live on-air interview for their 6:00 p.m. newscast describing the May 9, 2016, hailstorm and its impact on my neighborhood. I took a photo off of the TV screen later that evening as I watched the interview and posted it on social media with the following statement: "Interesting how I spent forty years doing drive-by photography of other people's storm damage and today I had the Channel 7 News reporter show up on my front porch to take photos of my neighborhood and do an interview. Seems only fair to have the tables turned."

CHAPTER SEVEN

I "Heart" the Great Plains

Chapter 1 of this book described in detail how my professional destiny was to live on the Great Plains and experience the extremes in weather and climate that frequent this part of our country. It has been a destiny fulfilled. I have watched so many of my University of Nebraska colleagues reach retirement age and then be faced with the decision to either remain here in the Lincoln vicinity or flee to another part of the country after retirement. Some of my colleagues who stayed here after retirement were very happy with that choice, others not so much. Some of my colleagues who left the area in search of retirement happiness far from the plains were content with that decision, others not so much.

As a geographer, I knew what I needed to do prior to retirement, and that was to travel to and explore all fifty states and the District of Columbia to see what activities might be of interest to me and what environments and weather and climate made me feel the most comfortable. I gathered multiple maps and planned four car trips that would take me to the forty-eight conterminous states, a fifth car trip north to Alaska and, finally, a sixth trip to Hawaii by plane. It was only after I arrived in Hawaii that I discovered that I could have driven to Hawaii. That sounds strange, but it would have only required my driving to Long Beach, California, and putting the car and myself on

62. The Center for Great Plains Studies' I "Heart" the Great Plains campaign. Photo taken in Montana by Daniel Clausen.

a freighter that would have, several days later, dropped me and the car off in Hawaii.

The advantage of residing here in the central Great Plains was that it was easy to explore all forty-eight states in four separate trips during four summers. Had I lived in any of the four corners of the U.S. it would have been awkward to keep returning home to that corner after each exploration, and the thought of seeing all forty-eight states on one trip would have seemed like a daunting task. I received my PhD at the University of Toronto, in Canada, so as a geographer, I thought it would also be interesting to visit all of the Canadian provinces and territories, which I partially did on our trip to Alaska and completed the summer we traveled to the northeastern U.S.

When I returned home after each of these trips exploring the U.S. and Canada, the important question that I asked myself had two parts: Do I still feel the most at home here on the plains? Have I found anywhere else that tugs at my emotions as a potential place to call home once my work life has transitioned into retirement?

I tried, I really tried, to fall in love with the Southwest. The warm mild winters with ample sunshine seemed alluring until I worked there on a drought project during midsummer. I loved the open spaces and endless skies but the heat beat me back. I never felt like I could adapt to that summer heat, and the most profound objection I had was the lack of green. Once I returned to the plains, I was overwhelmed with the rolling hills of green along with the green of the trees. It was even green along the interstate median as I traversed the plains toward home. I realized that I need a summer green landscape; the desert Southwest was unacceptable. It is a wonderful place to visit (maybe not in the summer) but it would never be my home.

The Southeast has, in my experience, two major drawbacks; the first is that it has far too many trees. I know Nebraska is the home of Arbor Day and trees are an important part of our landscape in the plains. And trees serve a very useful purpose as a shelter belt and they can make a river valley look very scenic. However, there are so many trees in the southeastern U.S. that you don't have many open views of the sky. It is virtually impossible to watch storms develop, to chase and photograph storms in this environment. The inability to observe the horizon and see a colorful sunrise or sunset with all the trees in the way is frustrating. The second drawback is that it has a climate that produces months of stagnant hot and humid air masses during the summer. When I have traveled to this area during the summer the air feels so heavy that you can almost cut it with a knife.

The Northeast is definitely high on the scale of beautiful scenery, especially in New England. However, the main drawback in this area is persistent cloudiness in the winter and much too frequent snowfall. Their summers are amazing, relatively cool and with much more sunshine than winter, but the prolonged dreary winters would make me feel very depressed.

The Northwest always takes my breath away whenever I have visited during the warm season. Snowcapped mountains, rushing mountain streams, and incredible viewpoints greet me along almost any highway. However, the drawback here is that during the summer, it truly is America's vacation playground with hordes of tourists bringing a crowded urban feel to the wilderness. I would not have the courage to live in the Northwest during the winter knowing that frequent heavy snowfalls can block the few access roads for days, isolating residents in their homes.

Although Hawaii was beautiful and lives up to its reputation as a "tropical paradise," it just didn't seem like paradise to me. Hawaii seemed like the ideal place to have a vacation, with its year-round tropical climate, but it also had no change of seasons, which I so embrace. It just didn't make me feel as comfortable and at home as I am in the Great Plains.

Finally, my hometown of Chicago always emotionally pulls at me and I make frequent trips back there with my family and more recently with grandchildren, taking them to the world-class museums, going sightseeing and shopping. But even though it feels like a comfortable pair of old shoes and I am comfortable exploring the city and driving on congested freeways, after about a week or so I begin to long for the Great Plains and my home back in Nebraska. One of my grandchildren said she loved going to college in downtown Chicago but she also felt claustrophobic and longed for the open spaces back home here on the plains.

What do I love about living on the Great Plains? Here, in no particular order, is my list:

1. **The wide open skies of the Great Plains**

   The sky is huge here on the plains, with open vistas providing perfect viewing of any kind of weather, especially developing storms.

63. Winter wheat ready for harvest in the Great Plains with a wide open sky filled with alto stratus clouds. Photo by the author.

64. Sunset on the Great Plains with red light reflected in a nearby marsh. Photo by the author.

65. A rainbow arches across the sky following a thunderstorm in the Great Plains. Photo by the author.

2. The sunrises and sunsets of the Great Plains

I have seen many sunsets and sunrises around the U.S., but I contend that they are the most brilliant and photogenic out here on the plains.

3. The rainbows of the Great Plains

I know that there are rainbows following spring and summer storms throughout all of the U.S., but just like sunrises and sunsets, rainbows seem to be more vivid and photogenic out here on the plains.

4. The four distinct seasons of the Great Plains

I really look forward to the change of seasons. Each of the four seasons has its beauty out here on the Great Plains and I equally embrace all of them. It is truly a "Goldilocks climate," not staying cold for too long, not staying too hot for too long, not staying dry for too long, and not staying

66. Spring on the Great Plains. Photo by the author.

67. Summer on a farmstead on the Great Plains. Photo by the author.

68. Fall is the peak time for harvesting corn on the Great Plains. Photo by the author.

69. Winter scene with a barn surrounded by patches of snow on the ground on the Great Plains. Photo by the author.

wet for too long. The extremely variable weather and very distinct seasons of the Great Plains keep the weather from being monotonous or boring. I love that first cold morning in autumn after the warm days of summer, the first snowfall of winter, the reawakening of the landscape in spring with all the many colors bursting forth, and the green summer landscape of the plains.

5. **The small-town culture and history of the Great Plains**

I've enjoyed exploring the small towns throughout the Great Plains with their genuine and welcoming residents. So many of these towns have small cafés that serve as a community gathering place and offer amazing food and, if you take the time to listen, some incredible stories about life on the plains. The Great Plains is a wonderful place to explore your ethnic heritage. For example, there are Czech, Swedish, Russian, German, Polish, and Italian communities across the plains that celebrate their heritage with community festivals.

6. **The annual bird migrations of the Great Plains**

There is a large variety of birds that use the Great Plains as a flyway in their annual migration. I have watched in awe year after year as the Sandhill cranes make their annual migration along with many other interesting types of birds. I live on the rural edge of Lincoln and each morning around sunrise, all year long, resident (i.e., nonmigratory) flocks of Canada geese lift up from their overnight stay in the nearby farm fields flying low over my home with their distinctive honking sound. They spend the day at nearby ponds and then the show is reversed just before sunset with the geese flying low over my house and landing into the nearby farm fields. When I am lucky, this morning or evening show is combined with a nice red sunrise or sunset.

70. Wilber, Nebraska, calls itself the "Czech Capitol of the U.S.A."
Photo by the author.

71. Sandhill cranes flying northward over the Great Plains. Photo by
the author.

72. The Platte River near Grand Island, Nebraska. Photo by the author.

7. The clean air and clean water of the Great Plains

I grew up near the steel mills in Chicago and our snow was often gray in color due to all of the particles of pollution falling from the sky. When I moved to the Great Plains, I so enjoyed the bright blue skies and relative lack of pollution. I have canoed several rivers in Nebraska and visited numerous recreational lakes and I never felt worried about wading in the water.

8. The Great Plains: It's an emotional thing

When you love someone or something, you can try to explain why you feel that way in an analytical manner. But most likely you will be lost for words after listing a few reasons and will just make the comment, "I just do, that's how I feel." I could list many more reasons why I love being on the Great Plains, but none of them can explain the emotional decision that tugs at you and says, "This is my home and where I belong."

73. Welcome sign at the Nebraska-Colorado border on I-76, October 2017. Photo by the author.

So here I am, where destiny has brought me, living and working on the Great Plains for over four decades. And I might add, with no regrets. However, retirement is on the horizon.

So where do I go from here when I retire?

When I arrived in Nebraska for my first job following graduate school, the sign "Nebraska . . . the Good Life" greeted me, and all these many years later the same message appears at the Nebraska border. Looking back over my career and my life living on the Great Plains and in Nebraska, I would have to disagree. Nebraska A N D the Great Plains are not simply the "good life." It is better than that. They offer the "perfect" life for work, play, and retirement.

To answer the question "So where do I go from here?" the simple answer is . . . nowhere.

The Great Plains has embraced me with all of its wonder, and for me it is now a lifelong commitment to remain here where I belong: I "heart" the Great Plains.

BIBLIOGRAPHY

Harner, Ariana, and Clark Secrest. *Children of the Storm: The True Story of the Pleasant Hill School Bus Tragedy*. Golden CO: Fulcrum, 2001.

James, Edwin. *Account of an Expedition from Pittsburgh to the Rocky Mountains*. 2 vols. Ann Arbor MI: University Microfilms, 1966.

Kooser, Ted. *The Blizzard Voices*. Lincoln: University of Nebraska Press, 2006.

Laskin, David. *The Children's Blizzard*. New York: HarperCollins, 2009.

Lavin, Stephen J., Fred M. Shelley, and J. Clark Archer. *Atlas of the Great Plains*. Lincoln: University of Nebraska Press, 2011.

Lawson, Merlin P. *The Climate of the Great American Desert: Reconstruction of the Climate of Western Interior United States, 1800–1850*. Lincoln: University of Nebraska Press, 1974.

Simmons, Laurie R., and Thomas H. Simmons. *Pleasant Hill (Towner) School Bus Tragedy Intensive Survey Plan, 2012*. Denver: Front Range Research Associates, 2012. http://www.kiowacounty-colorado.com/rpt-pleasanthillplandraft.pdf.

Stockville Women's Club. *Stockville, Then and Now*. Stockville NE: 1999.

Wishart, David J., ed. *Encyclopedia of the Great Plains*. Lincoln: University of Nebraska Press, 2004.

GREAT PLAINS WEATHER AND CLIMATE INTERNET RESOURCES

American Meteorological Society: https://www.ametsoc.org
    Professional meteorological organization

Center for Great Plains Studies: https://www.unl.edu/plains/
    Study of and appreciation for the people, cultures,
    and natural environment of the Great Plains

Climate Prediction Center: http://www.cpc.ncep.noaa.gov/
    Long-range, weeks to months, climate forecasts

High Plains Regional Climate Center: https://hprcc.unl.edu/
    Climate data and climate maps for the High Plains Region

Lightning Explorer: http://thunderstorm.vaisala.com/explorer.html
    The Vaisala Group's map of current lightning activity worldwide

National Drought Mitigation Center: http://www.drought.unl.edu/
    Drought monitor maps and drought historical data

National Centers for Environmental Information:
    https://www.ncdc.noaa.gov/
    Historical climate data

National Center for Atmospheric Research: http://weather.rap.ucar.edu/
    Current weather data and maps

National Oceanic and Atmospheric Administration:
    http://www.noaa.gov/
    Daily weather forecasts, severe storm
    warnings, and climate monitoring

National Severe Storms Laboratory: https://www.nssl.noaa.gov/
  Focuses on understanding severe-weather
  processes and improving forecast tools

National Weather Association: http://nwas.org/
  Professional meteorological organization

National Weather Camp at UNL: http://go.unl.edu/weathercamp
  Week-long camp for teens to explore weather and climate careers

National Weather Service: https://www.weather.gov/
  Current weather conditions and forecast maps

National Weather Service Forecast Offices:
  https://www.weather.gov/jetstream/wfos
  Map showing the local NWS offices for the Great Plains

NOAA Photo Library: http://www.photolib.noaa.gov/
  Large archive of historical weather photos

Satellite Images:
  https://www.star.nesdis.noaa.gov/GOES/GOES16_CONUS.php
  Current satellite images

Tornado Project: http://www.tornadoproject.com/
  Tornado information, books, posters, and videos

Severe Plot: https://www.spc.noaa.gov/climo/online/sp3/plot.php
  Make your own maps of historical severe-weather occurrences

Storm Prediction Center: http://www.spc.noaa.gov/
  Current severe-weather outlooks and severe-weather climatology

Wind Maps: http://hint.fm/wind/
  Current animated wind speeds and
  directions across the Great Plains

INDEX

Missouri: hailstorms in, 47, 48; temperature extremes in, 15; tornadoes in, 110–11
Missouri River flood: in 1881, 85–86; in 1952, 87–88; in 1993, 93–94
Montana, temperature extremes in, 17

National Wind Institute, 121
NDMC (National Drought Mitigation Center), 79–80
Nebraska: blizzards in, 63–65; hailstorms in, 44, 47–51, 50, 52, 52; ice storms in, 70–72, 72, 74, 74–75; lightning strikes in, 40; precipitation extremes in, 77, 82–83, 87–89, 88, 92–96, 95, 96; temperature extremes in, 4, 4, 5, 7, 10–12, 13, 14, 21–22, 22, 23, 24, 26, 26–27, 27; tornadoes in, 101, 112–39, 128, 134, 135, 136, 138
nocturnal vs. diurnal tornadoes, 104–5
North Dakota: blizzards in, 63, 65; lightning strikes in, 40; precipitation extremes in, 76, 77, 82, 90–92, 91; temperature extremes in, 6, 7, 7, 8, 24, 24
Northers, 9

Oklahoma: hailstorms in, 44, 48; lightning strikes in, 40; precipitation extremes in, 77, 82; temperature extremes in, 7, 12–13, 14, 15; tornadoes in, 101, 109, 110, 110

Omaha, Nebraska, tornadoes (1913, 1975), 112–18
Operation Hay lift, 64
Operation Snowbound, 64–65
orographic thunderstorms, 33–34
oxbows, 91

Pearson, David, 86
Platte River flooding (1993), 92–93
Pleasant Hill School bus tragedy (1931), 57–63, 60, 61
precipitation: Dust Bowl (1930s), 80–84, 81, 83; extreme variability of, 76–79, 77, 78, 79, 84–85; frequent Red River flooding, 90–92, 91; Lincoln, Nebraska, flood (2015), 94–96, 95, 96; Missouri River flood (1881), 85–86; Missouri River flood (1952), 87–88; National Drought Mitigation Center (NDMC), 79–80; Republican River flood (1935), 86–87, 88; Stockville, Nebraska, flood (1947), 88–89; two-part Nebraska flooding (1993), 92–94; types, 70. See also blizzards; hailstorms; thunderstorms
property damage. See damage

rain. See precipitation; thunderstorms
records: of hail size, 51–53; of temperature highs and lows, 6–7, 7, 15, 22–24, 23, 24

Great Plains Weather
Kenneth F. Dewey

Great Plains Geology
R. F. Diffendal Jr.

Great Plains Politics
Peter J. Longo

Great Plains Bison
Dan O'Brien

Great Plains Literature
Linda Ray Pratt

Great Plains Indians
David J. Wishart

Discover the Great Plains, a series from the Center for Great Plains Studies and the University of Nebraska Press, offers concise introductions to the natural wonders, diverse cultures, history, and contemporary life of the Great Plains. To order or obtain more information on these or other University of Nebraska Press titles, visit nebraskapress.unl.edu.